Making Friends With
The Boogeyman

Transforming Tragedy
Into Triumph

Heidi Smith

What they're saying about *Making Friends With The Boogeyman*

"In this powerful book, Heidi Smith shares how you can transform tragedy into triumph. The blend of Heidi's personal stories with practical exercises makes this book both intimate and useful. Reading this book is like having Heidi as your own personal coach and champion. Highly recommended!"

Aurora Winter, MBA bestselling, award-winning author of *Turn Words Into Wealth*

"WOW! This book was so moving and uplifting. I sobbed through parts of it and felt deeply seen and touched as a reader by Heidi Smith's story. I appreciated its authentic vibe, down-to-earthness, humour and humanity. The story is enjoyable and at the same time thought-provoking, mesmerizing, sad, loving and uplifting. It's so encouraging. It inspired me to let go of a piece of my own baggage. I'm grateful I read it."

Emily R

"Heidi Smith was a cheerful and lighthearted child who frequently made those around her laugh. But one night, when she was only 12 years old, this carefree lightness of being was buried alive. Heidi was half asleep, stumbling toward the living room, searching for her mother. What she witnessed left her scared to the core, and for most of her life, she carried the pain in silence and crucified herself for what happened. For many years, Heidi thought drinking and drugs were the only ways to escape her pain. But this would always create a pile of reasons to hate herself. In *Making Friends With The Boogeyman: Transforming Tragedy Into Triumph*, Heidi Smith guides us through how she overcame her traumatic past to become the best version of herself and how she discovered happiness in the wreckage.

Put down your sword and reconcile with your past. This was the message that stuck with me as I read this book. As human beings, we all have humiliating and painful pasts that we wish to lock away forever. Heidi Smith shares her story in a style that makes you feel and understand that you are not alone. She goes deeper to make you feel that you are so much more than your painful past. She incorporated several uplifting quotes that will leave you thankful you have made it this far. My favorite was the one that encourages the reader to always be optimistic about themselves. *Making Friends With The Boogeyman* is written from a first-person perspective. This made me feel as if I was sitting across a table from the author. This book will be a gift to anyone suffering from depression and wishing to see life in a new light. Psychologists and therapists will also find it beneficial to them in their line of work."

Readers' Favorite Five-star review from Alex Ndirangu

"Heidi Smith tells her story with humour and an open and courageous heart, inviting her readers to dive into the undulations of a life lived boldly despite some very rocky terrain. A journey into the beauty life has to offer when met head-on with vulnerability, strength, determination, and passion."

Jennifer V

"Breathe, this is how I felt after I finished Heidi's book. I felt I could breathe through my challenges, change my life and face my own versions of the boogeyman! Heidi bravely tells her story of recovery from addiction and trauma. She shares all of it with vulnerability and courage and doses of humour. Watching her transform through self-appraisal, hard work and curiosity took me on a journey I could not put it down; Heidi is a gifted storyteller. There is lots of practical advice woven in through the pages of her story. A must-read for anyone who wants more in their journey of life and hope in seeing how better is possible!"

Heather M

"Powerful Proactive Prose ~
In this raw and captivating biographical journey Smith shows that recovery is not only a possibility but can be a reality. *Making Friends With The Boogeyman* is a must read for those who are struggling with overcoming pain and suffering along their own journey. Smith's story will guide and inspire you on how to take back your power by reconciling the past, and reclaim well-being through Accelerated Evolution. Get ready for a great read. Embrace your journey, a great choice and wonderful gift to give yourself."

Lyn Bull

"*Making Friends with the Boogeyman: Transforming Tragedy into Triumph* by Heidi Smith details her experiences with alcoholism and drug abuse. Through her first-hand account, Smith encourages her readers to take steps to empower themselves and go down the road to recovery, turning to their strengths to create a fuller physically, emotionally, mentally, and spiritually secure life.

Heidi delivers the raw details of her story and the milestone event that led her to start using drugs and alcohol. Although she experienced embarrassment due to some of her actions, Smith moved on to empower others by sharing her experiences. The author's story is a candid testimonial, and many individuals would benefit from the honesty that flows from her words. Smith truly cares about her readers and understands their challenges. Through creative and personal channels, the author shows that her transformation was part of a process, and it led her down the road to a higher understanding.

Heidi Smith's dedication to her readers is clear, as she provides exercises to help them evaluate their feelings and try to process them more constructively. QR codes throughout the book help to clarify her points and provide readers with enrichment. *Making Friends with the Boogeyman* is a great book for anyone who struggles with substance abuse issues, as it shows that they are not alone. The book would be a good companion for other readers, as Smith's story could help soften their perspective on loved ones who may be struggling with the daily demands of life on top of tackling their dependency issues."

Readers' Favorite Five-star review from Courtnee Turner Hoyle

"Heidi Smith's *Making Friends With The Boogeyman* is an inspirational book for readers who want to transform their lives and live their dreams. Sharing her experiences with addiction, anxiety, and trauma to back up her message with concrete details is a great way to convince readers that she knows what she's talking about. Heidi Smith is also a Transformation Guide and Accelerated Evolution Coach so there's no doubt as to the credibility of this book. I find her tips for a successful transformation helpful. You should be willing to try something new, commit to taking action now, and believe that better is possible. I highly recommend this book!"

Readers' Favorite Five-Star Review, Marie Victoria Beltran

Published by Free Yourself Live Your Dreams, November 2022
ISBN: 9781738740000

Editor: Trevor McMonagle
Proofreader: Natalie Martin
Typeset: Greg Salisbury
Book Cover Design: Emily Rain Verscheure
Portrait Photographer: Kelsey Goodwin

DISCLAIMER: This book is not a substitute for professional help, medical, psychiatric or psychological diagnosis, treatment or advice. Readers understand and agree that they are fully responsible for their well-being. Readers of this publication agree that neither Heidi Smith, nor her publisher will be held responsible or liable for damages that may be alleged as resulting directly or indirectly from the use of this publication. Neither the publisher nor the author can be held accountable for the information provided by, or actions, resulting from, accessing these resources.

For my readers:
You deserve every happiness. I admire your courage in
reaching for something more.
From my heart to yours.

Table of Contents

Foreword

In your hands, you hold far more than a book. You hold a path from fear to freedom and illumination. As many of us know, it's fear that keeps us stifled, limited and playing small. We hold ourselves back by cowering to the inner boogeyman that feels real and has power over us.

Making Friends With the Boogeyman: Transforming Tragedy Into Triumph will not only show you how to conquer those inner barriers but will also explain how to transform them into your greatest gifts. Heidi Smith's moving personal story, along with her outstanding coaching skills, will illuminate the deepest and most lingering obstacles to your happiness, love and joy. You will experience her insight and warmth as you journey with her from tragedy to triumph.

Don't just read this book. Devour it fully and realize what your life is meant for. Take action and your fears will dissolve, your insight will sharpen, and your purpose will become supercharged.

I wholeheartedly recommend and respect Heidi Smith as a World Class Master Coach. Reading this book will show you why.

Satyen Raja
Founder WarriorSage Trainings
Founder Accelerated Evolution Academy

Introduction

Dear Reader:

Thank you for picking up my book. I wrote this for you. How did I know who you are? Easy. Either you are curious about my story or you are me where I used to be. If you're like I was, you are lost, desperate, frustrated, anxious and maybe even ready to give up. Only not quite yet.

You're a fighter.

You have been all your life; otherwise, you would have been dead a long time ago. There is a fire in you whether you realize it or not. It's what kept you going. It's the reason you keep trying when you feel exhaustion in your bones. I know that tired-in-your-bones feeling, when you are dragging your ass around. Sure, you look OK on the outside. You even look happy sometimes. Only on the inside a part of you feels empty, useless and lost. You've been to therapists and endless workshops, picked up what feels like a million books.

Maybe there are days when alcohol feels like the only escape from the hopelessness, the only way to cope with falling into darkness and self-hatred. Drinking and drugging can seem like the only ways to stop the relentless self-criticism going on in your head. If you don't succumb to drugs and alcohol, you have other tools for escape and distraction: working, binge watching TV, eating, shopping, exercising, or pouring yourself into others.

I hear you protesting: "Helping others is a good thing!" Absolutely it is, only I'm not talking about helping others. You and I both know the place where we disappear into someone else. When we go past all of our checkpoints of self-care to stretch ourselves so thin we snap. We burn out, become resentful, time becomes a distant memory until we end up crashing after pushing ourselves so hard that it may take days, weeks, even months to recover.

You and I are still here. We made it. I am a survivor and so are you! Many people don't make it. I know you've lost people. Me too. Maybe you've even considered checking out yourself. Only something stopped you. That grain of Hope, an infinitesimal spark of faith that there was something better. That spark has shone through the darkest night of the soul. In the most excruciating moments of chaos, it kept you alive. And now you are here, holding my book. I have stood where you are. Despite a lifetime of looking for something better, I still felt my life was in ruins…until it wasn't.

If you're curious, stick with me and I'll tell you how that all changed.

Acknowledgements

There are many people to thank for loving me through the journey of creating this book.

Thank you, Mom, for your fierce love. You cared for us and protected all of us even when we didn't understand. I feel your power always. Thank you, Dad, for being my cheerleader. You accepted me wanting to write this book even though it's not your thing. Thank you for your love and respect. Lilly, thank you for accepting this as well. You brought out Mom's playfulness. I see her joy and tenacity in you, a true mama bear. I love you.

To my beloved Mr. Smith, you have been my champion for all things. I am grateful for your faith in my ability to tell my story along with your belief in its importance. You stoked the fires of motivation when I needed it and remained patient when it took so long. Your attention to detail and instincts contributed to something we can both be proud of. Thank you for feeding my belly and my soul. You inspire me, you make me laugh, and I love you.

Dearest Lynderella, you've been in my corner from the very start. Thank you for being my biggest fan. I admire your light and the way you raise the vibration for all. Thank you for your excitement about this book and all my endeavours. Your experience, reflections and questions were priceless.

Thank you, Aurora, for reawakening my dream to write a book. I'm grateful for your guidance and holding me accountable for that first draft. The book has come a long way, baby! Angela, working with you changed my life. I will be forever grateful for your extraordinary coaching and introducing me to Accelerated Evolution. Our friendship is precious and I learn from your leadership, love, humour and self-care. When my commitment to the truth wavered, you reminded me the difficult stories needed to be told. Dearest Diane, I am inspired by your faith and courage, asking the hard questions and always speaking the truth with love. Who knows if I'd be a coach without you? Thank you, Dhyanis, for allowing me to hold you and witness your writing process as your book unfolded. You inspired me and kept me in the game. Thank you, Junie, for your love, guidance and expertise to reshape this book and for coaching me to let go of the Rebel.

Thank you to the late Zivorad Slavinski for your passion and generosity, creating innovative processes to share with the world. Satyen, I am grateful for your pursuit of knowledge, care, power and joy. I celebrate your brand of leadership with respect and adoration for the Divine Feminine along with the way you inspire us all to be our best selves. It is an honour to be part of your Accelerated Evolution Academy. Suzanne, you are a force of nature full of love, passion, creativity and joy. Thank you for teaching about Feminine Leadership and the importance of self-care. To my teachers Linda, Juan, Wesly, Jim, Andrew and Juliette, thank you for your dedication to this work and your fierce love for the students. To my Master Coach community, it is a joy to be in practice with you and celebrate our expansion.

To all my Beta readers, I am touched that you took on this project – the LONG version. You gave me the most precious gift of your time and attention. Eric, you always said I would write a book. Thank you for your faith and magnanimous feedback. Jen, thank you for your eagle eyes, vulnerability and making me laugh in the middle of your insights. Judy, thank you for your unique perspective and the pearls you shared. Heather, I have learned so much from you. I am grateful for your friendship and valuable reflections on this book. Thank you, Tannis, for your inspiration. You were brilliant, with endless love for everyone else bursting out of your tiny body. I miss your snorts of laughter. Emily R., thank you for relishing this book and the powerful uplevelling you shared. Emily O., thank you for your passionate encouragement.

To all my Mount Doug walking buddies, so much feedback was shared along that trail; thank you, Alex, for your curiosity and generosity. You never tired of the questions. Patrycja, I am touched by your fierce love and joy, the way you make us all family. Zara, when you surrender to your boundless joy, it is music for the world. We've walked this path a long time. When I was lost in those early days, you listened with the deepest love, sharing your experience to guide me onward, thank you. Denise, you manifest unlike any other. Thank you for your support of my calling.

Rebecca, you are a force of nature and I marvel at your accomplishments. Sven, thank you for your faith in me. You embody joy and strength. Together you two are changing the world. Thank you both for believing in me and celebrating my accomplishments.

Thank you, Greg, for your optimism and expertise. Thank you, Natalie, for your eagle eye. Thank you, Charmaine, for your generous guidance and enthusiasm. Trevor, working with you as editor was delightful. Your expertise, kindness, dedication and humour created a safe space inspiring me to tighten this book beyond what I thought possible. I am a better writer having worked with you and the reader has a better book. Emily V., my beloved illustrator, you are wise beyond your years. You pulled this cover out of both my darkness and my light, creating an image that said everything I wanted to say without me knowing what it was.

My heart is bursting with love and gratitude for each of you.

Lastly, to all the men in my life, especially my tall drink of water, you remind me everyday of the love, power and kindness of the enlightened masculine. Bless you all for proving my new story.

PART ONE
Tragedy

Emotions Are Energy In Motion

Unexpressed emotions will never die. They are buried alive and will come forth later in uglier ways.

Sigmund Freud

I remember seeing *Star Wars* for the first time. It was 1977 and I was eight. My cousin, who was ten years older than me, used to take my sister and me to the movies. I loved the movies in the theatre with the screen larger than life. I could disappear into the story, go on the roller coaster of emotions and adventure. I'm one of those people who buys into a movie, body and soul. I jump when I'm scared, I cry when I'm sad and cheer when the good guy wins.

This first viewing of *Star Wars* was my introduction to energy, to The Force. It was magic and it bestowed Ben, Luke, Leia and Darth Vader with extraordinary powers. Growing up Catholic, I heard plenty about extraordinary power, about the devil and about how my sins could damn me to hell. I was terrified by pictures of demons torturing humans in the red underworld. My parents hung wooden pictures of Mother Mary over my door so I would feel protected. That was my understanding of power. Then in my teens at a gas station I found a book with this improbable title: *Star Wars, Star Trek And the 21st Century Christians*. It prompted me to consider ideas from the movies alongside my religious upbringing. Growing up with the Holy Spirit, I was fascinated by this new perspective. What if the Force was available to all of us?

It's fun to look back at my childhood and see these innocent beginnings to my understanding and use of The Force. As I write this section, I am fifty-three and at peace with the power of my emotions. As a child I was afraid of the anger, hatred and fear that made up

3

"The Dark Side." When my mom was angry, I could feel the invisible power of it, that dark, scary energy. Although it's much easier to remember the dark, there was light energy as well. When joy filled our house, it felt light, bright, open and easy.

As I got older, the ferocity of the dark energies became stronger. A sensitive being, I was easily consumed by terror, hatred and fury. I had the same forceful temper as my mother. When the anger came, it felt like a storm: I needed to go into lockdown in the cellar. My earliest coping mechanisms were all about shutting down the larger-than-life, overwhelming waves of feelings that came over me. The safest place to be was in my head and out of my heart and body. It would take decades to unlock the buried emotions and free myself from the suffering my escapism had left me to deal with.

I was afraid of anger. Growing up, there were many booming voices, but even more profound was the intensity of the energy behind the voices. I could feel the outrage even when it arrived in silence. As I got older, my experiences fueled my own fury. The torture was that I had no idea what to do with it. I learned to push it down inside of me, having no idea how much I was hurting myself. Through many years of care, investigation and learning, I have allowed myself to integrate all that pent-up anger. Along the way I have educated myself on healthy ways to express my anger.

By far the most powerful shift after giving myself permission to feel my anger was the realization that my anger was actually a gift for me. When I recognize I am feeling angry, I now know that this is my body's way of telling me that something is not right with myself, with someone or with something else in the world. I am missing something I need or I've noticed something outside myself that I want to change. I consider anger nature's motivator; it gives me that potent burst of energy to take action. What a relief for me to accept my anger as a part of me, a collaborator for my highest good.

My hero's quest for peace from the mayhem of my childhood started in my teens. It has been a long and thorough process of investigation and experiential learning to move me safely back into my body. Today I am grateful to feel safe in my body, able to experience my life force along with the energy of others flowing inside me. These days I accept the visceral experience of all my emotions, recognizing that all my feelings are here for my highest good. It is my saving grace to recognize that allowing myself to feel the dark side—things like shame, fear and anger—is the path to freedom. Gone are the days I shut down to protect myself from the storm. Now I know that even my darkest emotions have a message and a purpose to improve my life. Today I welcome these messengers.

I accept fear as a part of me, knowing that it is trying to protect me. Just like a child pulling on a pant leg for attention, it has something to tell me. I'm no longer the child hiding under the covers, I am the powerful woman standing tall with a story to share.

My Dream For You

My thoughts go back to the year I was forty-one. I was experiencing a confusing, even painful, contrast of happiness and aimlessness. In my career I felt at the top of my game. For the first time in my life I was in a loving relationship with the man who is now my husband. For the first time I was experiencing the joy of electric chemistry with a loving match: a kind, intelligent man of integrity with a sense of humour, and he was sexy. This feeling of realizing my relationship dreams shone the spotlight on a shutdown feeling I had been pushing aside. What would it be like to know my purpose? I was itching to realize a feeling of fulfillment.

In the middle of all this wonder and joy, I would fall into an empty, lost feeling that didn't make any sense. I interpreted my emptiness to be a lack of purpose. It drove me to meet with new coaches and dive into new explorations until I discovered the block to my complete happiness. Making the unconscious conscious with the help of my guides transformed my life.

I want to talk about one of my coaching client's transformations. Let's call them Alex. As so often is the case, they started with the intention to work on one subject but as we spent time together, they connected with deeper issues they needed to address.

They began coaching with me after the death of their father. I've noticed that life-altering events like a milestone birthday, loss of a job, early retirement, divorce, a new relationship, or the death of someone close will often motivate individuals to seek my support. An event that shocks them into their mortality causes them to take stock of their lives and reflect, "Is this as good as it gets?"

I could relate to Alex being at a crossroads. They were feeling the heavy grief of a deep loss. The spotlight this shone on their life prompted them to contemplate, "What am I doing?" and forced them to look at their behaviour. Did they want to stay on the same path or do something different? Not changing would certainly be easier. However, they didn't like the version of themselves they saw waiting at the end of that path.

We had done some work together before and they had watched me continue in my personal development. (A wise friend of mine says, "If you're not moving forward, you're moving backward.") They decided to reach out to me and we began coaching together again. It was a tumultuous start. There were stumbling blocks with health issues, Covid and dark emotional times. This all culminated in a "Come to Jesus" moment when I reached out for my check-in at the halfway point of our coaching time together. Things didn't seem to be getting much better and they were inspired to drop their emotional kimono and reveal exactly how dire their situation was.

I am grateful they had the courage to be brutally honest about what was happening, despite their fear of disappointing me. I learned all I needed to know to tighten the container of love and support for them. Their raw feedback made it crystal clear what needed to change. We stepped up the support from biweekly to weekly calls with daily check-ins. They reignited their commitment to the process and became adamant about following through with their action steps.

As I mentioned, a common pattern with clients is to begin exploring one issue, and then once they experience the safety and care I provide, inevitably there will be blocks to continuing our coaching. There can be physical or emotional challenges that arise. It's like their deeper issues are needing attention. After seeing this pattern play out with multiple clients, I recognize that resistance is a tool for insight into my clients' needs. When we do something new, often we don't know what we need. Resistance tells us what we need to feel safe. Resistance is a blessing that allows the deeper sense of honesty required for deep personal development

I am in the business of changing lives. People seek me out when their old ways are not working and they crave something new. I guide them through clearing and cultivation. First, we clear the emotional charge, detrimental thinking and patterns around their challenges.

Then my clients create new patterns and behaviour from their insights. They choose the new thinking that rises from the clearing of emotions like anger, fear, shame—whatever was holding them back from the happiness and love they were craving.

When my client made their new commitment to go all in, they realized a transformation beyond what they had imagined. They experienced a loving reversal of darkness into light. It was a miracle for me as well, the first time that I perceived their shift in my own body.

They had kept their faith in the process; the miracle happened. They went from being exhausted, not wanting to get out of bed, to being energized and excited for what the day would bring. They realized their goal of letting go of the choking anger and resentment, and learning a healthy way of emotional management.

Now all their relationships benefit and they feel more joy in their life. They care less about what others think of them and more about what they think of themselves. What a relief, not caring about the burden of being what others want you to be. They put that down and haven't picked it up again.

They raved to me about the permanence of these changes. They had done plenty of different types of personal development in their life. Sure, they had experienced changes before, but nothing stuck. After thirty years of suffering from depression, at last they were feeling their light. We celebrated their new way of being, knowing the shifts they had made meant these changes were everlasting.

The way this client's transformation felt in my body was precious. When they were expressing all they'd experienced, I was picking up on their energetic transmission in a deeper way than ever before. I could feel their heart expanding. I went from flashing back to their time in the darkness, their anguish of being crushed into a small dark place and having no escape to feeling their love bursting at light speed as we spoke on Zoom. Limitless love and light brought tears of joy to my eyes.

How is that possible, you may ask? It's possible because we are all connected. I know the potential transformation as I have felt my own heart expand and expand. I've gone to that place where everything is love and we are all the same and there is nothing to be afraid of. It is light and peaceful and it is beautiful.

Everyone has their own experience of Oneness. Once you've been there, it is easier and easier to go back. I am grateful to have been chosen to facilitate change for others. It is worth every tear I have ever cried, all the agony, fear and anger that has racked my body. It has all prepared me for my purpose, to guide my clients to their truth.

I had the courage to walk the path to freedom and now I have the pleasure to show you the way.

This Is A We Program

And acceptance is the answer to all my problems today. When I am disturbed, it is because I find some person, place, thing or situation—some fact of my life—unacceptable to me, And I can find no serenity until I accept that person, place, thing or situation as being exactly the way it is supposed to be at this moment.

Acceptance Was The Answer from *The Big Book Of AA*

I remember hearing, "This is a we program," when I first started going to Alcoholics Anonymous (AA). People talked about what was happening in their lives through the lens of not drinking and the Twelve Step principles. Everyone had a chance to speak for up to five minutes uninterrupted. People in the room listened quietly, without judgment. From an early age people have come to me to confide their deepest secrets so in that first meeting I was comfortable listening to other people's stories. I was also amazed at the depth of honesty and vulnerability. The level of raw authenticity moved me to tears. My own pain and anguish were being spoken out loud by stranger after stranger.

I remember a lady talking about how, when she first quit drinking, she was certain that she would never have fun ever again. Her story immediately grabbed my attention.

I wanted to shout, "That's me! That's how I feel. How in God's name am I ever going to have any fun without booze?" This was a life-or-death question for me. She spoke of how she connected with people in AA. She told stories about all the potlucks and deep friendships she had found. She remembered the first time she came to a meeting and heard deep belly laughs. There were people having fun and she wanted that badly. She had captured my attention and provided the hope and inspiration to keep me from drinking that day. As well, she ignited a hunger in me to keep coming back and learn more about this place, the people here, and how they had fun without drinking.

Her story gave me hope. It gave me a path. It gave me a plan of action. As I watched the people of AA, I did what they did and my life was transformed. I am grateful to say I had and still have the belly laughs I was promised. The greatest thing about my new belly laughs is that I remember them. They stay with me and the joy from those moments is in my body and accessible at any time. It is a stark contrast to the empty, disembodied laughter from my drinking and drugging escapades.

In that first meeting I witnessed living examples of the happiness and connection I yearned for so desperately. That's what I wanted and so I chose to continue not drinking each day. I changed my thinking and actions until I had the same incredible life I had heard stories about. I didn't know what was possible until someone else showed me. Once I saw it done by someone else, I gave myself permission to do the same. This works for me in all areas of my life.

Drinking had been my escape and my solution all in one. It took a stranger to tell me that, in fact, drinking was the reason for my disaster. My drinking and the chaos I created with it were magnifying my hopelessness and misery.

The lessons I've learned along the way eased my suffering with addiction, anxiety, depression, and destructive patterns from my painful past. Today I am free from those internal prisons because others took my hand when I reached out for help. Now I'm here to take your hand to show you a way to the peace and happiness I know exists. Keep your eyes, ears and heart open for everyone waiting to show you the way.

You are not alone.

Three Gifts For You

Three Gifts is a practice given to me by Satyen Raja, the founder of Accelerated Evolution, when I told him I was terrified that I couldn't help people as a coach.

> Accelerated Evolution is an integrated set of verbally-guided transformative experiences that allow anybody to dissolve inner conflict, emotional knots and stored trauma, allowing the natural emergence of peace of mind, flow and effortless peak existence.

 He explained to me that no matter how much I helped people, my ego would never believe it was enough. He said something like, "No matter what you do, there is always more to do. Don't let that stop you. Get out there and help people anyway." We talked about our core wounds and how they will never be healed. As coaches we are meant to use those wounds to serve others. Our purpose is to give others what we didn't get as children. Whatever I longed for and never got enough of as a child is now my gift to the world. Giving others the safety, love and truth I craved as a kid brings me relief.

"Conscious being with choice" is a foundational principle I learned from Raja. Our essence is perfect, whole and complete. There is nothing wrong with us. Each of us is aware of our surroundings, thoughts and sensations with the power to choose our experience. This is our unique journey and we don't need to be fixed. Whatever is happening in this moment is exactly as it is meant to be for our awakening.

I begin all of my coaching sessions with a breathing exercise, giving my clients three gifts: safety, love and truth. Before we get any further, I want to offer you the same. Take a moment here and do this with me.

Imagine that you close your eyes, and get comfortable in your chair. Take three slow, deep inhales through your nose and exhale out your mouth, letting go of anything that came before this moment. As you inhale, follow your breath into your body. Imagine feeling your seat in your chair. As you exhale, let go of any tension there may be in your body, and let go of anything you need to do after this exercise. Give yourself permission to be here and now, knowing everything that needs to be taken care of will get done.

The first gift I offer you is safety. You are not alone; we are all connected. Even though you cannot see me, I am here with you to love and accept you where you are. I have no judgement about you or anything you've done. I know you did the best you could at the time. In this book I'll tell you some of the most painful, humiliating things I've done and experienced to show you that you are not your past. We are all so much more than our painful past. I am here to show you that we are light and love.

The second gift I want to share is love. I love your curiosity. You are always open to learning something new, being exposed to different perspectives, experiences and ideas. I love your determination. If you're reading this book, you probably want to change something in your life. You are determined to feel better and you keep trying new things that move you closer and closer to your vision of a better life. I know you will keep doing something different until you get what you want.

The third gift is truth. A truth I see in you is that you already are everything you want. You already have all the answers to the questions burning inside you. David Pomeranz says in his song, *It's In Every One Of Us To Be Wise.* My hope is that things you read here will help you remember the incredible being you already are.

Lay Down Your Sword

Growing up, I experienced relatives getting drunk, bellowing and fighting. I remember needing to shut out that yelling, banging and lashing out. None of it made any sense to me. I remember one time lying on my stomach on the floor absorbed in a TV show. I didn't realize a drunk uncle was trying to get my attention so he thought I was ignoring him. He proceeded to slap me hard on the bum. It shocked the hell out of me. There was no rhyme or reason to it and I learned that at any time I could be attacked.

My nervous system was constantly on high alert even long after I left home. The distrust and defensiveness became my way of living. I created a life strategy for protecting myself out of the beliefs and behaviours created in reaction to shocking childhood incidents. Unfortunately, that unconscious programming ran my life for decades.

I was fiercely independent. I was so angry with life that I trusted no one, not even myself. I had absolutely no respect for authority and when I was directed to go left, I went right. When it was suggested that "It would be good for me to…" in defiance I always did the opposite. That kept me going. I even had a certain pride about it. I was my own person, or so I thought. In reality, I was a puppet for the fear, anger and hatred locked up inside of me.

The only way out of that prison for me was surrender. However, I never surrendered until I was beaten down, exhausted and desperate for something different.

Maybe you know what that's like. I invite you to open up to the love and support around you. Once you lay down your sword and make peace with your past, you will be amazed at your transformation.

It may be the case that, as I tell you my story, you find some events and language I use disturbing. It may even be the case that you find yourself feeling triggered by the subject matter, feeling agitated or anxious. In that feeling of discomfort you may want to run away, lash out or shut down. I get it. That means it's time to take care of yourself. I recommend you don't fight these feelings. Instead, imagine that these feelings coming up are a good thing. What's happening is your feelings are trying to tell you something.

Accept what's happening and take a break from reading in order to soothe yourself: focus on your breath, look at your hands while you clench and unclench your fingers, all the while reminding yourself that here and now you are ok. Journal about how you're feeling in order to explore what's coming up for you. Talk with someone you trust about it. Take care of yourself, go out into nature, play with your pet, get a hug from your partner or friend.

At the back of this book in "Resources," I share some simple exercises to bring you back to the present if you are feeling triggered. You haven't done anything wrong. My experience is that my baggage shows up when I'm ready to unpack it. Timing is everything, and when I'm strong enough, that's the time challenges show up for me. Today, I deal with my challenges one day at a time and pace myself. I am grateful to realize that I don't have to do it alone and neither do you.

I was compelled to write this book because I've learned that transformation is beautiful. I believe that everything happening in my life is for my awakening, even the ugly, painful stuff. My journey has taught me how to embrace what's going on with me and learn from it to enjoy my life more. That is what I want for you.

It is important for me to tell the truth. Growing up, I was starved to know what was going on around me. My parents were European and their position was that "Children are seen and not heard." That meant I was often the last to know what was happening. I remember being confused between what I saw going on, what I was told about what was going on, and what I felt was going on. Over time I let the adults in my life talk me out of trusting my intuition that was telling me what was going on in the silence of what wasn't being said.

Today I worship the truth. Throughout these pages I offer you what happened in the most real way I know. I want you to understand from my experience that no matter how hard things get, there is a way through. I've done it and so can you. On the bright side, I tell the truth not only about the painful, ugly things that went down but I also do the same with stories of the good things in my life and the strange, goofy ways I've lived and learned. Come along as I tell the tale of making friends with the boogeyman and how this helped me to find happiness in the wreckage of my past.

The Never-ending Nightmare

*If you change the way you look at things,
the things you look at change.*

Wayne Dyer

I plan to take you on a journey from violence, anger and hatred to celebration, self-empowerment and love.

I ask that you prepare yourself to hear stories and language that you may find shocking and uncomfortable. In writing this book, I challenged myself to feel my narrative as fully and deeply as possible, the same way I challenge my clients to dive into their emotions and experiences to "Unlock their blocks." If you're anything like me, you have a powerful imagination and care deeply for others; hearing someone's story can feel like torture. If you find yourself reacting to the story, perhaps feeling agitated or overwhelmed, listen to your body and make time for some self-care to get grounded: take a break, stretch your body, drink a glass of water, get something to eat, go outside, do some breathing exercises, give yourself a hug, whatever you are craving. Only within the last ten years have I begun to respect how deeply I am affected by the pain and emotions of the people around me. That awareness, a miracle for me, enabled me to begin to care for myself in ways that exponentially decreased my suffering.

Before I found ways to navigate my intense emotions, my primary coping mechanism was not to feel them. I did what I could to shut down emotions or escape them with alcohol, drugs, TV, shopping, eating: whatever worked at the time. My life has been all about moving from my head back into my body and heart. It's been about learning to accept myself: everything I've experienced, all my choices. Everything. The more I practice self-acceptance, the more I connect with myself and experience the joy and wonder in life.

My story begins with a happy, light-hearted kid. I would make up songs and sing them on the way to school. My sister and I sang songs on road trips, we danced, we made up plays. I was often acting goofy and making my family laugh. I had an active imagination and my sister and I made up all kinds of games together. There was no Internet, no cell phones. All the information I had was from my family, friends, oh, and TV.

I was a smart kid, meaning I was book-smart and did very well in school. I was naive and trusting, doing as I was told. My biggest fear was getting in trouble from my mom or any other adult. As children, we knew we were second-class citizens in our household.

I remember adults drinking a lot when I was a kid. I noticed everyone getting a lot louder and acting strangely. I never liked loud noises. They scared me. One thing I did know was that if I was quiet, the adults would forget about me and I could stay up late and watch TV or play with my toys, delaying the terrible nightmares I knew would come. Shutting out the adults to disappear into my own little world was my happy place. The walls could be falling down around me but if the TV was on, I was absorbed with whatever I was watching such as *Wonder Woman* or *The Bionic Woman*. Even though I was surrounded by chaos, my basic needs were well taken care of by my family. I had everything I could want or need because my mom and dad made sure of it. I had no idea of any money problems. For me things just magically appeared.

That carefree lightness-of-being vanished when I was twelve.

Now, I think of my childhood night terrors as the price of having an active imagination and being a sensitive soul. Back then I was simply terrified of the dark. I remember feeling so uncomfortable in it, so alone like something was coming to get me. It drove me to get close to someone, like my mom or my sister in order to get some sleep. When I woke up in the night and my dad was out of town, I would go to sleep with my mom for comfort.

For a time, we lived in a basement suite. I hated that place. It was dark, dingy and unlike the nice house we lived in before. I know now that we moved there because it was impossible to find anything else to rent at the time.

I remember waking up one night in particular. The floors in the bedroom were made of cold plastic on top of concrete and they sent a shock through my system when my bare feet touched them. I shared a room with my sister who was blessed with the ability to sleep through the night. Dad was working out of town so when I woke up I did the usual and headed for Mom's room.

The apartment was pitch black. I am nearsighted and see even worse in the dark. I stumbled into Mom's room, trying not to wake up fully. Only she wasn't there. "Huh, maybe the living room?" I thought. A long hallway from the bathroom to the living room passed in front of all our bedrooms. I stumbled back into the shadowy length, feeling my way around until I plopped myself onto the couch of the living room in total darkness. Bewildered and still half asleep, all I wanted was to find my mom, my safe place from the Boogeyman.

And that's when I heard her…crying. Thinking back, I imagine my eyes opening even wider and bulging out, trying to see more in the darkness. My ears strained to hear what was going on. I couldn't see anything. I didn't call out at first because maybe I would get in trouble. I leaned forward towards her voice, hoping to hear what she was saying. She was whispering, I guess, to keep from waking up us kids, but her crying whispers were determined and crystal clear.

"NO! Don't! Pleez stop it. No! Stop! You'll wake the kids."

Shock rushed through me like an electric current. Pins and needles shot through my head.

I didn't want to believe it. I had seen enough TV movies to know my mom was being raped right there, right in front of me. Maybe two or three feet away where she was pinned down on that ugly, puke-green carpet. I hated that carpet. It was an uncomfortable floor covering that failed miserably at its sole purpose: to provide warmth and comfort from the concrete below. There was no comfort from that rug. I panicked. Without knowing why, I ran to the bathroom. I felt terrified, confused and sick to my stomach. I had no idea what to do. Back then, I was a scrawny kid who was shy and didn't say shit if my mouth was full of it. What chance did I have to stop this horror?

The centre of my life was under attack. The only man in the house was violating my mother and I was powerless to prevent it. If she was afraid to fight him, what on earth could I possibly do?

RUN!

I sprinted for salvation.

Noise!

I thought to myself, "If I make noise, he'll stop, not wanting to wake the kids." I turned the light on in the bathroom. I flushed the toilet with the door open and then I scurried to my room and leapt into my bed, pulling up the covers tight to my chin, my heart pounding in my ears, happy to hear anything instead of what was happening to my mother down that long, dark hall. Totally panicked, alone in my bed while my sister slept and my dad was away, I felt the tears well up and silently roll down my cheeks into my ears.

Terrified, I lay frozen in my bed. What I wouldn't have given for all this to be just a bad dream. Maybe, if I just kept still, the Boogeyman wouldn't get me. I made what was happening out there feel far, far away. I was furious with my dad. Why wasn't he here? Why couldn't my sister wake up? Why did I have to be alone? What was happening to Mom? I wanted to scream but somehow I couldn't. Instead I lay silent, swallowing my sobs and clutching my blanket, my teary eyes clenched shut while I prayed to God,

"Why is this happening? Pleez, make it stop."

I stayed like that all night until I passed out from praying for it all to go away.

I slept in the next morning and was late for school. I never even heard my sister get ready and leave. I went into Mom's room where she was sleeping. When I tried to wake her, she pulled her arm up over her eyes, looking to escape the punishing sunshine. She had no intention of getting out of bed. Knowing what I know now, I'd say she was painfully hungover. Physically and emotionally sick from all that transpired the night before. Her only directions for me were, "Leave me alone and get ready for school."

I went back to my room and did what I was told. The next thing I remember was going into the kitchen and experiencing the outrage of finding him relaxed at the table.

HIM!

He was sitting there drinking his cup of coffee, comfortable as you please, like nothing had happened. It was one of Mom's "buddies," someone she partied with. I think his name was Freddie. I remember his sandy, curly locks and a pudgy face with thick lips. I refused to look directly at him so the details are dim. As I write, I am stunned to realize his shady details had been the face of the devil in my nightmares for years after.

I was thoroughly and completely disgusted by his presence. I didn't have the words to express the enormity of what he had done to our family. Everything in my body was screaming for me to get out of there so I ran out of the house as quickly as I could. I remember speed walking to school and talking to myself along the way, trying to make sense of everything that had happened. My head was filled with images and sounds, spinning with rage, confusion and disgust, creating a debilitating concoction of torture and devastation.

My mother and I never talked about what happened that night, not ever. My mom died in 2017 so I'll never have a chance to hear in her own words how that event impacted her. I know that for myself, carrying the secret of that incident completely changed the course of my life. I was convinced I had let her down and spent most of my life crucifying myself for that ultimate failure.

That night slammed the door to my childhood and annihilated everything innocent and naive in me. The smiling little girl who danced and made jokes was buried alive by the ugliness, fury and loathing from what happened. I hated men, the kind of hate that makes the bile rise up from your stomach and burns your throat. I decided that all men were pigs who would rape you if they thought they could get away with it. The power of that makes me shiver even now. From that night on, the world wasn't safe and I needed to keep my guard up.

It was a rite of passage launching me, years later, on a desperate quest for any escape from the extreme emotions that resulted. I dove into personal development workshops, courses, books, and was fascinated with all things to do with self-improvement. I made many breakthroughs with my confidence and my communication skills; however, I had little success dealing with my intense emotions. I was fearless in my experimentation and would try anything new to feel better about myself, constantly looking for different tools to address all the rage and hatred that ran my life. Despite everything I learned through the years, I often felt stressed, tense, overly serious, lost and hopeless. All I wanted was just to relax and forget. I was searching for anything that would stop the incessant analyzing, hearing the perpetual diatribes of criticism and self-hatred in my head.

I began to use alcohol and drugs more and more as coping mechanisms. Reaching for them as a sanctuary became automatic. All the while, unknowingly, I created a self-destructive pattern that was making things worse instead of better. Of course, my sanctuary of drinking and drugs was a lie, creating shameful, disgusting behaviour that contributed to a mountain-high pile of reasons to hate myself. In the end, all that mattered was the anguish of my childhood fading into a dark hole in my chest, forgotten.

Words Have Power

Why am I writing this book?

I am a writer. It has been a hell of a journey, going from trapped to transformed, from victim to victor, moving from contemplation to exploration and expression. All my life, I thought I needed someone outside myself to validate my worth. If I was a good daughter, sister, aunt, student, employee, then I was worth something. The old story was that I needed to have a degree for people to listen to me. I say "old story" because now I write my own adventure. In fact, *Write Your Own Adventure* was the starting title of this book. I am a cheeky little monkey and I'm having fun with writing my story. Why?

Because I can and you can too.

If you are a seeker like me, you have been on the road of personal development for years and this isn't your first rodeo. You've likely had a fascinating life and I suspect that plenty of it was painful. I am here to say my freedom came when I changed the way I looked at the pain. The transformation was and is in the way I look at the events, not in the events themselves. That's why I say, "the old story."

I have learned that our words have power. They are the choices we make. They are the perspective, the lens through which we view the world. What feels like a million years ago, I read *A Return to Love* by Marianne Williamson. The ideas were magic to me. They were old ideas from *A Course in Miracles* and no doubt had been written earlier elsewhere. That didn't matter to me. Reading Williamson's words was the first time I had heard these concepts. They changed my life. About the same time, I remember hearing another important idea from Wayne Dyer: "If you change the way you look at things, the things you look at change."

I was exhilarated with these ideas. They were empowering, and my mind was exploding with the possibilities. I remember walking around clutching the Williamson book, thinking I held the secrets to the Universe. And, well, I did.

The happiness of your life depends upon the quality of your thoughts.

Marcus Aurelius

It's simple. How we think dictates how we feel. Thoughts become feelings and stories—oh my goodness—stories! The old story I told myself about writing a book was that I needed a degree to be a writer. That was a way I devalued myself and my ideas because I didn't have a degree. I have wanted to write a book ever since I was a kid. It's only happening now in my fifties. Why did it take this long? I needed to think I could write a book and people would be interested enough to read it.

It has taken me this long to realize the value of my experience. The value of my perspective. The value of sharing the way I finally found peace and fulfillment after more than three decades of suffering. Now I have peace, bliss and purpose. That is worth sharing.

That's worth writing about. That's worth facing all my fears to get this book to you, my reader. Facing fears about the critics who could say, "Who the hell do you think you are?" or the haters who might come after me on social media, people laughing at me because they think I am ridiculous. All those crazy fears. When I found a way to free myself from suffering and lead an extraordinary life, I wanted to shout it from the rooftops.

So here I am shouting, "I DID IT! I DID IT! I FINALLY DID IT!"

Words Make A Difference

Practice:
to perform or work at repeatedly so as to become proficient

Merriam-Webster Dictionary

One of my favourite words is "practice." This concept was offered to me in a yoga class to illustrate how every day that we come to the mat is different. Some days we feel good about what we are doing, other days nothing feels like it went right. Yoga teaches that the outcome does not matter. All that matters is that we come to practice. It's a word often used in yoga, or meditation. I now use it for everything: writing, work, life.

Eighty percent of success is showing up.

Woody Allen

For me the hardest part is showing up but I do it anyway. I give it the best I can in that moment and let go of what happens after that.

Using the word "practice" about my yoga relaxed my entire body. It gave me permission to stop beating myself up about how crappy I thought I was doing, and just be. What a relief. That is the reason I started using the concept of practice everywhere. For example, writing practice means a commitment to write. My job here is to take action and do the daily work.

My process is to let go of the outcome. I learned from Julia Cameron that what comes out of the work is not my department. My job is to show up every day and write, letting go of the expectation of whether the writing is good or bad. Using the perfect word sets the stage for our mindset and our actions. When I say something like "I am a crappy writer," I immediately start to feel bad about myself. I judge my abilities. I start to procrastinate about writing. That all adds up to me writing less, which threatens whatever project I'm working on.

Notice the impact that words have on your feelings. A key that I found liberating is the change from the words "I am sad" to "I feel sad." I expect that you've heard this before. In the first statement, "I am sad," there is no separation between "I" and "sad." They are one. It is far more difficult for me to feel better when I am one with sad. The second statement is, "I feel sad." Here, there is separation. I have some control, I can choose to feel sad or not feel sad. The ability to change how I feel becomes more possible. Even though it sounds like a crazy mind trick as you read it, I invite you to try it and experience the difference for yourself.

When I say "I am angry" with my husband, that stokes the fire of my emotions and angry thinking. I am one with the anger and I don't know how to get out of it. When I say "I feel angry" with my husband, there's room to move around. I can ask questions to shift the feelings. I can ask questions like, "What's going on with me? How long do I want to feel this way?" Feeling angry sucks, especially when you are an expert, like me. I learned from generations of women who were ignited by rage like a match by a flint.

My mom was the kind of woman who inspired the aphorism, "Hell hath no fury like a woman scorned." For most of my life, I identified with that. My temper would fly out of control with yelling and throwing things. Once I stopped drinking, the outbursts lessened, only the intensity continued with long silences, while the rage boiled inside. Thank God for writing! Oh, the journal entries I've written. Oh, the many pages on which I've purged all my venomous thoughts and feelings to save myself and my relationships.

Understanding words and their power can be our salvation.

The way I talk to myself and about myself also impacts the way I think and feel. Once I know that I have the power to change my words, which change my thoughts, which change my feelings, I become the master of my destiny.

The most powerful example of this is what happened to me when I was twelve years old, witnessing my mother's rape. Rape is a visceral word, a violent, gruesome, devastating word that takes us on a mental journey. People use it less nowadays. The new phrase is "sexual assault." I used to think it was the watered-down version, a softer, gentler way to describe the offense. The "kinder, gentler thing" pissed me off for a long time.

In my mind it was a way to sugarcoat the offense so the perpetrator didn't look as bad. That was when I was stuck in my rage. Saying the word "rape" over and over kept me in my fury and hatred. It felt awful every time I said it. Now I see that the word upgrade to "sexual assault" is actually for the benefit of everyone. Thinking about the words "victim" and "trauma," I have realized they too need an upgrade.

Victim:
one that is injured, destroyed, or sacrificed under any of various conditions

Merriam-Webster Dictionary

This is a word that strips you of your power. When you say, "I am a victim of..," you identify with the injury, destruction and sacrifice. How does that feel in your body? For me it was like the weight pulling me to the bottom of the deepest, darkest hole I could find. I was powerless over what had been done to me. Now I realize I had accepted this identity of victim almost unconsciously.

When I was a child, I had no idea what else to do with the intense experience; I had locked it away with all the shame and anger I felt. I hated myself because I did nothing to save my mom. I was engulfed in the fury of my situation and all I wanted to do was lash out at everyone and everything. That's what I did, over and over. For decades I was trapped in reliving the emotions from that night. I had no idea how to make peace with what happened so I locked it away, leaving it to subconsciously wreak havoc with my life. It was many years later before I came to recognize that seeing myself as a victim meant I was still being held hostage by what happened. Seeing myself as a victim made me my own cage-maker.

Survivor:
a person who continues to function or prosper in spite of opposition, hardship, or setbacks.

Dictionary.com

What happens when you replace the word "victim"with "survivor?" "I am a survivor of..." Try it and notice how that feels in your body.

I know I feel stronger when I have survived something. It is over, it is in the past, I am moving on. Once upon a time, survival for me was only about continuing to function. Now that I know how thinking about a situation shapes my experience, surviving is about thriving. I practice choosing my words to shape my thoughts and perspectives. Today I feel myself prospering from the devastating things I experienced in my life. With my new thinking and the work I've done to move through the fierce emotions from crippling experiences, I am free from the torture of my past.

What It Used To Be Like: My Addictive Escapades

Drinking alcohol was always a big part of our family life. In our European culture, it was acceptable for children to have a bit of wine on special occasions. When I was nine years old, I went to visit my grandma in Europe. This led to a major celebration since it was the first time my mom had been back home since she was nineteen.

My grandmother had started purchasing cases of Henkel Troken, a sparkling wine, as soon as she heard the news that we were coming for a visit. By the time we arrived in December, her bedroom wall was covered floor to ceiling with cases of wine. The night we arrived, we were the honoured guests at a huge party with live music, dancing and free-flowing booze at the Community Hall.

My introduction to my mom's brother was the two of us in a chuggalug contest, furiously gulping down the sparkling wine. I have a very competitive spirit and it never occurred to me to hold back. I was determined to drink as fast and as much as I could, unaware of what it meant for my young body. It only occurred to me to stop drinking once I had the spins and had to lie down on a nearby wooden bench. I never threw up. That should have been a warning sign that I was different. I had my first blackout on that trip. For some people, their memory eventually returns. That has never happened for me.

When I was in my early twenties, I remember partying with my friends at the bar. We were all wasted. When the bar closed, we decided to head to my place to keep drinking. There was a guy I liked in the group and I remember following him outside when he left the party to puke in my yard. Somehow I was still irresistibly drawn to kiss him, vomit breath and all.

I didn't remember anything else from that night when I woke up the next day about 4 p.m. in my bed, wearing different clothes than I was wearing the night before. My head was exploding and I was painfully nauseous. My whole body ached. All I wanted was to retch and die.

Only I had to get to work.

I have no idea how I was able to do such a thing. All I remember is going very, very slowly. Shockingly, I got myself there even though I looked like death warmed over. Someone heard me vomiting in the bathroom and reported it to my supervisor. Once they took a look at me, they promptly sent me home.

I called my friends from a payphone in the mall for the play-by-play of the night before. Barely able to stand, in a cold sweat, I crawled into the mini cubicle of the public phone, and dialled the number for my childhood friend. I listened to his depiction of how I had stripped down naked and was determined to run downstairs to seduce the fellow that I had kissed earlier. It was everything my friend could do to keep me in the covered stairwell of my sister's three-bedroom condo, away from the view of our other friends. He reported to me how he had struggled and pleaded until, finally, he got me back up to bed, and put some clothes on me. Then they had all left.

Listening to him, I was desperately searching my memory for any details to disprove his story. My heart sank when I could not retrieve even one shred of evidence to disprove the story of the humiliating escapades he was sharing with me. My memory jumped from kissing the guy outside on the patio to waking up and going downstairs to find the kitchen clean, with all the dishes in the dishrack. These were good and kind people. They had invited me into their crowd before they knew I was an asshole. I hung up the phone, racked with shame and guilt, deciding then and there that I would never see them again.

I slithered home, a shell of the person I used to be, and crawled into bed, desperate for the oblivion of black unconsciousness.

This was a recurring pattern for me. Time after time, I alienated myself from the latest group of drinking buddies when my boozing got out of control. It was easier to find another group to hang out with than it was to deal with the mortifying spectacles of my drunken alter-ego. I was longing for people who wouldn't judge me. Rather than address my drinking and the deterioration of my social behaviour, I craved belonging to a gang that would accept me as the reckless waif I had let myself become.

I remember one time moving in with the latest group of friends who partied with bikers and used crack cocaine. They partied in a new neighbourhood with fewer rules and there was no judgement in that crowd.

The good news for my drunken alter-ego was that my new group spent far less time out at the bar and far more time at home, with the shades down and our drug of choice in the open. Another upside for me was that I didn't get all crazy using crack cocaine. I didn't black out. It was a very soothing drug for me. Being someone whose mind was always racing with punitive recriminations and venomous pangs of self-hatred, I was frantic for a complete break from the agony between my ears. The crack gave me quiet, and things moved slowly in my mind. I listened and watched everyone around me like they were far, far away. There was no attachment or emotion to what they said or did. I remember smiling or nodding because it was required. Thinking back, I realize that I just wanted the respite from the constant internal attack, and more crack, of course. It was always about more.

This became the routine... Come home from work about 7 p.m., make something to eat and then count the hours until the drugs arrived.

I was fascinated by my friend "cooking" the coke. Fixated by every move she made, I told myself I was learning how to do it. Only it wasn't anything that practical. No, watching her was like some sick kind of foreplay, a mix of keeping my eye on her so she didn't cheat me out of my share of the drugs and a vulgar anticipation of getting stoned again for the precious moments of relief from everything I'd been through. Then, once the coke was prepared, I had to endure the torture of waiting for that first hit. First, there was the measuring out of the ice-coloured pebbles for each of us. Next, we gathered around the dining room table for more waiting, each taking our turn on the pipe. Round and round we went, smoking our brains out until all our crystals disappeared. It was hazy, yet sadly, not hazy enough to dim the bright lights of the chandelier. A dimmer would have been a godsend. There was always some conversation, usually convoluted stories from our flamboyant hostess. Even though I often found myself losing track of what she was saying, I made a point of showing interest and trying to keep up with her. It was a difficult undertaking since all I really wanted was to be lost in not caring about anything.

Once we ran out of drugs there was the inevitable discussion of whether we could get more. That all depended on what time it was and how much money we had. Once we exhausted all options for extending our freebase bender, each of my roommates quickly disappeared to their own room for privacy and respite to nurse the misery of all the drugs being gone. Brutal. My mind was slow when I was first stoned, only that didn't last. Once the narcotics disappeared, my thinking quickly picked up the pace again and I couldn't sleep.

What the fuck was wrong with me? How did I end up here again? Every night it was the same, tossing and turning alone in my room on my pathetic single bed, berating my behaviour, begging God for some sleep. Lying in the limited darkness before sunrise, I desperately pleaded over and over for some slumber salvation, my distress growing with the waking light until I finally passed out, an hour or two before I had to leave for work.

The morning after, I always bolted awake; it could be an hour, sometimes thirty minutes before my ride picked me up for work. Mornings were a blur of running around preparing my uniform, washing my face, brushing my teeth and trying to look presentable. Somehow I managed to get myself together in time for my friend to pick me up. I sat in her car, smiling and nodding to the conversation, barely conscious. The only thing getting me through was the thought of the coffee and breakfast sandwich waiting for me once we arrived at work.

The day was a blur of smiling and engaging with the customers, other staff and my supervisors at the casino where I worked. A rotation of forty-five minute shifts followed by a fifteen-minute break kept us all mentally focussed on our game. By the end of my day, I almost felt like a normal person. Everyone at work thought I was a "good girl." I was talented at looking clean-cut and proper, with nothing in my appearance to expose the drug fiend I had been the night before. My co-workers seemed terribly confused by my choice of friends. What was I doing hanging out with the black sheep and the outlaws?

When I was with people who thought I was a "good girl," I could never feel any real connection because of all the shame and self-hatred inside of me. I was constantly thinking, "They are too good for me." I was sure that if they had any idea of some of the things I had done in my life, even just the night before, they would politely pick up their drink and get the hell away from me. When I was with the drug crowd, I wasn't comfortable either because nothing felt real. All anyone cared about was drugs. None of the conversations or emotions were true. It was all about drugs and money or manipulations to get more drugs and money. It all seemed empty and tragic. Even when I got out of the drugs and went back to the drinking, there was no real comfort or connection.

I had to find other broken people like me because that was where I belonged. I went from being one of the cool crowd to clinging onto one single person who could relate to the anguish I'd been through because they had suffered too. It was the opposite of hanging out with successful people. I hung out with the traumatized. I hung out with the survivors who didn't have time for bullshit.

My best friend was always the one saying, "Screw you!" to the world. We were saying it together. I needed the fire of that "Rebel" mentality to keep me going, because staying in the attack position stopped me from thinking about myself. All my feelings had been pushed down so deep I was terrified at what would happen to me if they came back up. You would think those kinds of deep bonds would last forever. I was heartbroken to realize that inevitably the relationship blew up and I was alone. Back to walking through the crowds, searching for someone broken like me.

That was my twenties—a pretty girl on the outside, smart, easy to talk to, hard-working, but rotting away on the inside. It was simple to find a job because no one could see the inside, just the outside. It was uncomplicated to get along with the "normal crowd" because only I knew I wasn't what they thought. Early on, I accepted the loneliness of being surrounded by people who had no idea who I was. Looking back now I understand: it was me who had no idea who I was. I was obsessed with my darkness and completely blind to anything else. My image of myself was like the needle stuck on the record, skipping over and over in the exact same spot. I was frozen, stuck, shut down and oblivious to what was holding me back. It wasn't until my mid-thirties that I began to consider my stumbling block might be that I couldn't get over the night my mom was assaulted, the night I did nothing to stop it. On the outside, I was getting older, changing jobs, moving to different cities, finding friends and even having fun at times. Inside, my emotional development was crippled by my memories, drugs and drinking...lots and lots of drinking.

I had been living under a dark cloud, unable to breathe for so long that I was convinced I was damned to this life of loneliness and desperation. I hated myself. I was trapped in an invisible cage. I didn't know how to talk about it or who to talk to. I couldn't see any solution.

I was convinced there was something inherently wrong with me. I was broken. I was defective. I was alone, completely unlovable, with joy becoming more and more of a distant memory. And that was my life for the foreseeable future. I spent my evenings alone in my apartment, pulling vodka out of the freezer, drinking to mindless TV until I passed out with that good ol' garbage can by my bed. I woke up just a few hours after passing out only to toss and turn until I got up to go to work, came home and did it all again. It was an interminable cycle, the revolving door of my feeble life going nowhere.

My Transformations

Transform:
to change in composition or structure
to change the outward form or appearance of
to change the character or condition: convert
Transformation:
an act, process or instance of transforming or being transformed

Merriam-Webster Dictionary

Transformation is one of those glorious, big, mind-blowing words. It is an all-encompassing experience of moving from being one expression of a person, place or thing to being a completely new version of them. I am grateful to say I have had many transformations in my life. For the purpose of my life and this book, transformation is the perfect word. It elicits an image of someone morphing from one iteration of themselves to a new and different one. The next version of ourselves may seem to be a subtle change to the outside world but is in deep contrast to the profound inner experience.

When I look back on my life, three transformative moments spring to mind: a car accident, what happened to my mom when I was twelve, and my mother's cancer.

I was in a car accident in 2016. We were waiting on an off-ramp to merge onto the highway. The driver behind us fell asleep, inadvertently setting his car in motion to smash into our rear end. The powerful vibration of that impact moved through the metal of the vehicle, over my flesh and bone, through my spirit and emotions. In one instant a seemingly insignificant domino set off a chain of events I would not understand until years later. The fact that we call it a "fender bender" is an example of how we tend to downplay the tragedies in our lives.

The instant after the impact I felt different. I felt shaken and had a general experience of feeling "off." My husband and I went to a mediclinic to get checked out then later went to our family doctor to check in. I felt sore after the accident but the pain subsided after a few days. It was only months later that I began experiencing major headaches. Then in the following year I began experiencing severe pain in my right hip and leg, and brutal pain in my middle and lower back. It was a pain that over-the-counter painkillers didn't touch. The extreme discomfort sent me on a hunt for something to relieve the pain and get me back to my normal self.

Over a few years, I worked with a physiotherapist, a pain specialist named Dr. Greg Siren and a chiropractor named Dr. Michael Tucker. I didn't feel any relief with the physiotherapy; in fact, my experience was that the pain worsened from the agitation of the exercises while there was no overall improvement with the pain. Working with Dr. Siren, I experienced profound relief of my intense back pain after the very first visit. Before finding the Myo Clinic, I felt completely powerless over my physical body. Up until the accident, I had been healthy, free to do pretty much anything I wanted. It was a shock to have that freedom taken away from me so unexpectedly. Everything became about my pain levels. I even noticed the deterioration of my marital relationship, feeling loss of control over my emotional outbursts because of the intense physical strain. I learned about a new level of fatigue that affected me on all levels: physical, mental and emotional. Being the self-aware person I am, I was watching myself change before my eyes. With the long-term consequences of the accident, I got in touch with the vulnerability of my physicality.

My life changed so that everything was exhausting. Napping became a necessary coping mechanism. I was working from home at the time and mercifully, I was able to nap as often as I needed. Have a treatment, take a nap. Work a few hours, take a nap. Go for a walk, take a nap. I was learning a new level of acceptance with what I was capable of doing.

Working with Dr. Tucker, I began opening myself to the new body I was living in after the accident. His approach was not about fixing me or getting me back to normal, it was about accepting my new situation and working with my body as it was now. My work with him was about unlocking the opportunities in front of me. This question arose: What if my body was better than it used to be?

I was grateful for our spiritual discussions along with the physical relief his treatments offered. At the time we were working together, I was also exploring yoga as a healing modality. Between the two, I had a major epiphany about my pain.

In yoga and meditation we use the word "sensation." In my yoga classes I was prompted to feel what was happening in my body and go to the edge of that sensation. My teachers guided me to listen to my body, accept myself, and not push myself. I knew the practice of being with the sensation until it passed because of my experience at a Vipassana meditation retreat. That had been ten days of sitting, the daily sit routine broken only by meals, walking meditation, and sleep.

We would rise in the darkness to the sound of a bell and silently prepare ourselves to go to the pre-breakfast contemplation. Sleepy bodies emerged from the cabins for the morning march to the hall, moving through the floor maze of cushion concoctions for a full day of sitting. The intention was to sit in silence and, without moving, slowly scan our body for any sensation. When a leg cramp or some kind of discomfort arose, the goal was to notice the feeling, accept it, and keep our attention on it while keeping still. Many times there would be a building of intense piercing or throbbing until I was driven to shift my body for relief. Then there were the times when I was able to maintain my focus until the discomfort disappeared. Victory! I had the discipline to stay the course without giving into the distraction of my physical suffering. It was there that I learned the word "anicca," that is, impermanence. With the endless hours of sitting and chanting "anicca" to myself in the throes of excruciating aches or irritation, I nourished the physical embodiment of the wisdom that "Everything in life is impermanent." Eventually, this too shall pass.

Regular yoga classes along with my flashback to Vipassana fueled the exploratory conversations with Dr. Tucker about the word "pain." I made the transformative decision to practice using the word "sensation" rather than "pain." That word has the power to cause intense discomfort whereas "sensation" is a neutral word. It feels more open, giving the opportunity to experience without any preconceived notions. My sensations can be pleasant or unpleasant, intense or minor. This gave me a new freedom to interpret my experience. Once I changed my perception of the pain, the experience of the pain also changed. At last there was mental relief along with the physical relief. Although I still had sensations because of the car accident, once I changed the way I thought about them, my experience of them shifted. I realized that I had the power to lessen my physical suffering simply by changing my thoughts. Even with intense sensations, I learned how to be in my body and take back control of my experience. It was transformative.

I began seeing my car accident as a gift rather than a curse.

The repercussions of this fender bender still continue as I write this book in 2022. I am grateful to say I have a more intimate relationship with my body. I've learned to love and accept my body as it is rather than because of what it does for me. Today, I see the event as an opportunity for evolution. My choice today is to look at whatever happens to me and ask myself, "How could this be for my benefit?" or "What's the advantage here?" To me, life is learning.

The car accident resulted in a short transformation, although the progression it sparked is something that continues, as with all transformation. Life is in constant motion and we are continually changing, whether we see it or not. Although we may be able to pinpoint what initiates a transformation, the results are beyond the scope of our contemplation. The momentum lives on through our entire existence.

The car accident, like my mother's attack, was a potent reminder that our lives can be forever altered in an instant. A phone call has changed many people's lives forever. For me, that life-changing phone call, leading to my third transformation, came when my mother called to tell me she was diagnosed with terminal cancer. She was calm when she called. She had been sick for years and at last the doctors had a diagnosis to explain the extreme weight loss and physical devastation. Knowing this, I could not manage to care about the day-to-day matters. Sure, I had a business and I continued to work for my clients as a virtual assistant (VA), completing projects and meeting expectations. I did what I had to do, but my heart wasn't in it.

My grief kept me from feeling any desire, any purpose, anything. Living in the grief of my mother's impending death was the strangest existence. I witnessed the excruciatingly slow demise of the one who brought me into this world, the one who raised me, the one who gave me my DNA, the one who gave instruction on everything from how to wash myself to how to care for my husband. I learned consciously and unconsciously over the years observing her relationship with my father. The long-term exposure to the slow-motion death of my mother as she fought a battle she wouldn't win was a living loss that altered my psyche and my cells. The journey through her illness and her death was like her giving birth to me again, only this time I was the sole survivor.

Of my three transformations, the longest of my life began the night I witnessed my mother's attack. From that instant, I understood the violation I had witnessed. The shock of the violence penetrated my emotional, physical and spiritual body. However, as with the car accident, I was oblivious to how that one moment in time would shape me and continue to influence my view of the world. I became possessed by that quote, "What doesn't kill you makes you stronger."

The initial impact was utter demolition of all trust and safety. The world I lived in was defined by the savage man who brutalized my mother. It was my new truth that men could never be trusted. This man, someone she trusted, had exerted his own will with a detrimental disregard for her wellbeing. Selfishly and violently, he made himself more important than her. He completely demeaned her. She had no value. Her needs didn't exist for him. She was nothing. She pleaded over and over for him to stop, begging for herself and her children.

He never listened to a word she said. She had no voice.

Looking back through her life, I see how it killed her not to have a voice. To my knowledge, she never spoke about that incident. She carried the harrowing secret inside of her never daring to let it loose. The resentment was a bitter poison she swallowed, eating away at her. It took thirty-seven years until she contracted thyroid cancer, a cancer in her throat that infected her entire body, until her assasination was complete.

As I reflect on her silence, her not being heard, I am experiencing new insights and noticing interesting patterns. Many times in my life I have thought and felt, "You are not listening to me." I first took on this belief from my parents, and it was anchored in me after what happened to my mother. For years, I felt that way with my husband. An example of this was the endless disagreements we had about getting married.

I remember him telling me early on that he didn't want to be married or have children. We had been dating for about three months and we were getting serious. Out of respect, he wanted to be transparent about his boundaries in case I wanted children. He wouldn't want to get in the way of something so important. I have no idea how we got to this conversation but what I do remember is that when he said he would never be married, it was like someone punched me in the gut, hard. Everything was frozen in the shock of hearing those words. Up until that time, I had never wanted to be married. What I hadn't realized before that moment was that I had never been in love either.

The idea of not having children was not a shock to me. I had made peace with that idea when I was sixteen years old. After everything I had been through as a child, I vowed to myself that I would never have children unless I was capable of giving them an incredible life. That meant loving them deeply and making them my priority. I would have a stable home with a loving husband who would be a wonderful father. For me, having children was all about giving them the life I didn't have. I never had the desire to have children to love me; it wasn't about me. It was perfectly logical to me that if I couldn't give them an incredible life then I didn't need to have children.

Hearing Rob's disclosure, my choice was to bury my heart's desire to marry him. I told myself that all these intense feelings didn't mean anything, that I was overreacting.

Over the next three years, I did my best to forget about those feelings and desires, telling myself I was being ridiculous. Rob was an amazing man. He loved me and he was clear that he didn't want to be married. I loved him too and that meant being together without being married. The obvious solution was to push down any emotions trying to tell me otherwise.

As you can imagine, that didn't work very well. You can never silence your heart's desire. Eventually it will surface like the dandelions making cracks in the concrete until they rise, at last, to the sunshine.

Back then all I knew was that I wanted to be married. Trying to forget this need or minimize it or talk myself out of it wasn't working. At first I was afraid to say it. However, slowly over time, my confidence grew and with the help of some counselling I owned it. I gave myself permission to want it and then I said it over and over. I explained all the reasons it was important to me. The discussions went on and on. I felt like he never heard me. Not until the day I had had enough of not being heard and told him I was leaving him.

That, he heard.

What I realize now is that he had been hearing me but my words and my actions were not lining up. In my mind it was unmistakable that I wanted to be married. Yet, there I was in a relationship with a man who had definitely stated he didn't want to be married. I was complicit in disregarding my own dream.

It was only once I believed my own words and turned them into action that things changed for us. When I accepted that we wanted different things and that having my dream meant being willing to let him go, my heart and mind were finally in alignment. That is a powerful place to be and that's when Rob knew what I wanted and everything changed for us. Up until that point I was just talking. Actions speak louder than words and Rob always had the ability to tell himself I wasn't being serious because if I was, I would do something about it.

As with my husband, it confused me when others didn't value words the way I did. When I was a child and my mom said something, I listened. Then I witnessed a man overpowering my mother. My mother pleaded with him over and over, only it never made any difference. Her words didn't mean anything to him. All that mattered was what he wanted. Perhaps the story he told himself was that since she didn't fight, yell or bite, it meant that she wanted it too. Of course, she didn't want it. She was telling him over and over to stop. I knew there had to be a reason that she wasn't fighting. As a child, I thought it was because she didn't want to wake us kids. My mom was a powerful woman who always spoke her mind. As the night went on, I began to think he was doing something to her to keep her quiet. Was he threatening her? Did he threaten us? The fact that she wasn't fighting terrified me even more.

I've learned as an adult woman about all the judgement that survivors of sexual assault face over and over. I imagine what a nightmare this whole thing would have been for my mother to explain. I picture her being fire-hosed with fault-finding questions. How could this happen? What was he doing there? How much did you drink? Why didn't you make him leave? All of the questions had the underlying message that this was all her fault. Obviously, she did something wrong.

Why would I think that? Because I heard it over and over from family, acquaintances, and the news media. I remember having an argument with my dad when I was about nineteen. We were talking over a news story about a woman being sexually assaulted.

I heard him say something like: "She's drunk, it's her fault."

His words set me off like an atom bomb, and our conversation went along these lines: "WHHAAAATTTTT! Are you for real, how can you say such a thing? What the hell are you talking about? What about him? It's his fault, he's the one that attacked her. What the fuck is wrong with people? They are always blaming the woman. What about the asshole who assaulted her? Why isn't anyone blaming him, judging him! He was the one who couldn't keep his dick in his pants! He's the one who forced himself on her. He's the one who did something wrong, not her."

My dad said, "He wouldn't have been able to take advantage of her if she wasn't drunk."

"Oh my God! Are you serious? That's ridiculous. No means NO, whether you've been drinking or not. OK, what about if a woman is walking down the street at night and some guy jumps her and violates her. What then?"

"She shouldn't have been out walking alone."

"Jesus, Dad, that's insane! Do you have any idea what you sound like?"

I was getting louder and louder. That's when my mom burst in from the kitchen;

"Stop it, you two! That's enough!" She was speaking that strained voice of hers. It wasn't yelling but it was potent. It was like she was holding back a hurricane of hellfire and we all had better do what she said.

So we stopped the conversation and I stormed up to my room or out the door, anywhere to escape this demented exchange with my dad. My poor mom. Obviously my dad had no idea what had happened to her. I was defending her, except I was the only one that knew it. I was sick to my stomach with the fact that my mom had to hear all the hurtful things my dad said.

My dad is a kind and sensitive man. He never would have said such things if he had known what happened. What I understand about my dad now is that he didn't truly believe it was the woman's fault. He was looking for a way to empower all the women he loved to keep them from harm. If the reason a woman was violated was because she was drunk or walking by herself, then all she had to do to keep from being assaulted was to not get drunk and not walk alone. I know now that there is more love in this way of thinking than judgement.

When at last I confided to an older female relative what had happened to my mom, nothing was done about it. I was fifteen or sixteen at the time and still had no idea what action to take. Telling an adult did nothing to help me. All I had was rage and self-destruction; for decades I carried around the belief that I had no voice.

Using your voice is one of the most powerful tools you have. There's a synergetic relationship between thinking, words and actions. Transformation only happens when you have all three. It took me admitting that being married was my heart's desire before anything could change. Then I needed to speak it out loud as part of bringing it into reality. Lastly, it was necessary to physically do something to change my situation.

I remember being surprised by how light and happy I felt after we got married. My body felt like a screen that had been clogged with dust and debris stuck in it for years being washed clean for the air to flow through, free and easy. This freedom to know myself and use my voice was earned after countless years of self-sabotage.

Before that fateful night of my mom's attack, I was an honour student. I won the award for most outstanding student at my elementary school and was second runner-up for most outstanding student at my junior high school. After the assault on my mom, I had less and less interest in school and started skipping classes. At first it was nothing major, just Home Ec, and I would go home to watch soap operas with my mom. In Grade ten, I barely made the honour roll, and my disgust for men in power was building. In Grade eleven, I remember asking a male teacher a question in Math class. When I thought he was finished, I turned my head from looking at him back to looking at my homework. Apparently he wasn't finished talking because he walked over to my desk and put his hands on my head to turn my face back toward him.

How dare he!

I was livid. I remember thinking, "How is this OK?" You may be wondering what I did. Did I swear at him, call him on it, or maybe tell the principal?

No.

The action that made sense to me at the time was to quit that school. I finished the year and then enrolled at Alberta College, where all the high school graduates paid for courses to upgrade their marks for university. I was sixteen and working by then. Since I used my own money to pay for all my classes, it never occurred to me to ask permission from my parents. Everyone at the school was older than me, some as old as nineteen or twenty. None of the teachers cared if I showed up for class so my absences escalated, especially for the courses I hated like Math, Chemistry and Physics. As you can imagine, my school marks plummeted and I never graduated high school.

I had gone from a twelve-year-old hanging out with all the cool kids, at the top of her game, to someone hanging out on the fringe with one friend who was eccentric, also full of rage and disdain for authority figures. Even so, I never gave up searching for ways to feel better about myself.

My best friend's father at the time was an alcohol and drug abuse (AADAC) counsellor who ran evening workshops on things like Gestalt Therapy. It was all fascinating to me, and I was enthusiastic to attend. I was surprised when my parents were not as excited as I was, and I closed up, sharing as little detail as possible. They didn't understand what I was getting into and the whole thing frightened them because it was another change in behaviour on a long list that didn't make any sense to them. How could it? They were missing a key part of the story. Obviously they had no idea about my witnessing what happened to my mom. It's not like I was thinking about what happened every moment of the day. It was pushed way down inside of me, creating regular explosions of anger and contempt. My defiant behaviour was a mystery to them, and I have no doubt they missed the reasonable, affable child I once was.

It was a presentation on Gestalt therapy and conversations with older friends at work that led me to my first five-day personal development workshop. I was nineteen when I enrolled in the Omega Vector seminars. I dove in, taking level I and even travelled to another city for level II. It was a new world full of highly intelligent people exploring their feelings and transforming their lives, healing lifelong, heartbreaking experiences. I learned about communication, personal growth and self-awareness. I remember watching one of the workshop facilitators and thinking, "I want to do that!" I volunteered for the group, looking after things like registration, happy to be a part of the community. Everyone there seemed extraordinary to me. One of the fellows who had a major breakthrough in the workshop hosted a potluck at his home that had an indoor pool. In a city where winter could go on for six months, that was incredible to me.

Even with these positive influences, my self-destructive behaviour continued. My drinking was more regular and out of control. My conviction that authority was the enemy and never to be trusted continued to warp my perspective and my decisions. The minute my dad wanted me to do something, I did the polar opposite, automatically, without even thinking. I see now that many times it was to my own detriment. I had always considered myself an independent, free thinker, yet in reality I was controlled by a trigger created in me at twelve years of age.

Ways To Ease The Pain

Research shows that alcohol use and alcohol-related problems are influenced by individual variations in alcohol metabolism, or the way in which alcohol is broken down and eliminated by the body. Alcohol metabolism is controlled by genetic factors, such as variations in the enzymes that break down alcohol; and environmental factors, such as the amount of alcohol an individual consumes and his or her overall nutrition. Differences in alcohol metabolism may put some people at greater risk for alcohol problems, whereas others may be at least somewhat protected from alcohol's harmful effects.
National Institute on Alcohol Abuse and Alcoholism

I am a highly sensitive person and feel things deeply. The fury and hatred I felt for humanity and myself after the night my mother was assaulted engulfed me for years. I started drinking to get drunk when I was twelve. I am an alcoholic and my body reacts differently than a non-alcoholic person.

As an alcoholic I was addicted to drinking. I didn't have the same natural ability to stop drinking that a person who is not an alcoholic has. The most obvious difference between someone who drinks heavily and an alcoholic is that when the heavy drinker experiences negative consequences like losing their memory, losing their job or getting into fights from destructive, reckless, drunk behaviour, they will stop or cut back on their drinking. When I was getting into fights and blacking out, I just kept drinking. I continued ingesting alcohol long after I had blacked out.

> An alcohol-induced blackout is a temporary type of amnesia, according to an online article from Scientific American:
>
> In medical terms this memory loss is a form of temporary anterograde amnesia, a condition where the ability to form new memories is, for a limited time, impaired. That means you can't remember a stretch of time because your brain was unable to record and store memories in the first place.

My experience of a blackout is that I appear physically conscious, only "my mind has left the building." I have no awareness of my surroundings, words or actions. In a blackout, everything I do is unconscious and I do not remember it when I wake up the next day. So I did things like strip naked and try to run through my house party to make out with some guy. Thankfully, that time my childhood friend stopped me from completing my mission, only that didn't stop the shame of it.

My system was always on high alert because I believed the world was out to get me. I tensed my body and emotions like steel. The only time I let myself relax was with drugs and alcohol. Self-destruction became my playground and I spent more and more time there. I stayed there even though everyone who knew me was screaming at me to stop. It was like when the theatre audience at a horror movie is screaming, "Stop! Don't do it!" at the teenager going out into the forest, knowing damn well the poor sucker will be slaughtered. The person on the screen never hears the advice and neither did I.

Sobriety

The next type of transformation is something you consciously choose, like sobriety.

Sobriety. Thinking back to how I felt before I got sober, I would liken myself to the Pig-Pen character from the Peanuts comics. I was under an impenetrable black Cloud of Doom that followed me everywhere. It was the loneliest time of my life. I was drinking alone a lot by that time. My existence was always altered in that I was either drunk or hungover, never just normal. I was what they call a "functioning alcoholic." I managed my job and paid my bills. Well, sort of. Even though I was in massive debt and completely irresponsible with money, I still considered myself functioning since I hadn't lost my job, my home or had my electricity cut off. Everything was about feeling better. That meant not feeling the intense anger, loathing or tension that were my everyday experience.

I remember lying in bed realizing what my life was. I had a bucket beside my bed in case I needed to vomit in the night and couldn't make it to the bathroom. I was drinking alone and wandering the streets at night, drunk. My drinking friends had deserted me after a chaotic trip to New York where the group relationship shattered in the drama of drinking, lies and manipulation. Sure, I had other friends but none of them had a clue who I was. I felt like I was doomed to live this desolate existence forever.

Looking back now, I see how wrong I was.

I was telling myself all kinds of stories. That I was mentally ill. That there was something wrong with me. Never once did I consider drinking all the time could be the problem. Everyone who witnessed my drinking was telling me I had a problem. And I was telling them all to go to hell.

> Alcoholism: a chronic, progressive, potentially fatal disorder marked by excessive and usually compulsive drinking of alcohol leading to psychological and physical dependence or addiction.
> NOTE: Alcoholism is typically characterized by the inability to control alcoholic drinking, impairment of the ability to work and socialize, tendency to drink alone and engage in violent behaviour, neglect of physical appearance and proper nutrition, alcohol-related illness (such as hepatitis or cirrhosis of the liver), and moderate to severe withdrawal symptoms (such as irritability, anxiety, tremors, insomnia, and confusion) upon detoxification.
> Merriam-Webster Dictionary

Never once did I consider I may have been an alcoholic. That was blatant denial. Now it is inconceivable that I could have been so completely oblivious to my own alcoholism. I had witnessed many alcoholics throughout my life, raging alcoholics, depressed alcoholics, life-of-the-party alcoholics. People that were incapable of not drinking even when they were hurting themselves and others.

To me, it was obvious that I wasn't an alcoholic since I wasn't really hurting anyone. I was a single woman with no children. What did it matter if I drank myself into a stupor? I was the only one paying for it or not paying for it. I went to work, I met all my commitments, I didn't drive a car. So who was I hurting? I wasn't doing anything wrong, my drinking was my business. I walked around under my somber cloud never once considering that my misery, isolation and despair could result from drinking like a fish. It sounds crazy even as I write this. Back then I was so lost in the problem I couldn't see what was going on. I knew my life was a mess, only I kept drinking my way through the misery, expecting to find a solution. Not once did I ever consider that to stop drinking was the answer. That was someone else's suggestion.

I remember a dinner party with friends. A mutual acquaintance walked in the door. When I greeted him and looked into his eyes, they were filled with such peace and serenity I was shaken to my core. My existence was anything but peaceful. I was full of anxiety, self-hatred and hopelessness. I felt like a P.O.W. forgotten in a deep, dark hole, waiting for death. Then there was this surprise visitor, popping the lid to my cell, offering me a hand up, offering to show me the way out.

Without even thinking, I took his hand and did exactly what he did. That meant taking a workshop called Choices. I called and found out the date of the next seminar, conveniently only a few weeks away. I found out the cost. I didn't have the cash but that didn't stop me. I remembered I had some RRSPs (Registered Retirement Savings Plans) so I cashed them in. I was desperate to have what he had, pure and simple. In recovery, they call this "Going to any lengths."

There was no time for "I can't." My answer was 100% "I can!" The only questions I asked myself were How questions. How can I pay for this? How can I get time off work? How can I get there? (It was out of town). I was sick, sick to death of feeling the way I did. This Choices alumnus was well. He was serene. I don't think that I even knew I wanted to be serene until I experienced it in another person. There was a drastic difference between the anguish I felt inside and the soothing peace that washed over me when I looked into his tranquil blue eyes. It wasn't about what he said that night, it was about who he was. This was a pivotal moment in my life that snapped me out of unconsciousness. I was awake and paying attention.

There were four of us at that dinner party. Everyone at the table noticed the unmistakable change in him. Our hostess wanted to sign up for the program as well. That man inspired a lot of people to take that course. Choices should have paid him a commission. Now that I've seen a lot of transformations, I can say it has the most pure energy of attraction. It is nonverbal but undeniable, washing over you with the announcement that "if they can change, I can too."

I was committed and ready to take the leap without any details of what I would find when I landed. Sure, I had been through this kind of workshop before but it had been fifteen years earlier and a lot had happened to me since then.

Was I afraid? I must have been feeling some trepidation. Only I don't remember it now. My friend and I were on our way. The power of two is amazing; anything is doable when you have a buddy.

Then, the night before the course, I got a call that my buddy couldn't make it. They had some health issues and were under medical direction to stay off their feet. They felt terrible about leaving me hanging. I told them it was OK, and not to worry about me. I was used to going to things like this on my own. I would be fine. When I got off the phone, I sat in the living room of my three-storey walk-up, swivelling in my chair and contemplating how to get to the ferry in the morning.

I felt no anger or resentment towards them. Rather, I chose to accept their decision and move on with my plans. When I make plans with friends and something comes up so they need to cancel, I choose to accept it and wish them well. I never have any resentment or try to guilt them into doing what I want. I was and am a firm believer in the teaching of "Do unto others as you would have them do unto you." Nowadays, when something comes up for me and I need to reschedule with a friend, I always turn my attention to one of my foundational principles:

Whatever is for my highest good is for the highest good of all.

No matter how it looks at the time, I choose to believe this.

Growing up as a people pleaser and now adopting this perspective gives me permission to take care of myself first. I want the freedom to follow my heart without the pressure of pleasing others, which means I practice offering that same freedom to everyone I encounter, especially my loved ones.

A happy end to the story: My buddy ended up going to the Choices seminar the next time around with their mom, and they had a fantastic experience.

Sure, I was disappointed when they cancelled our trip. It certainly would have been easier if we had gone together. Alas, that wasn't the Universe's plan for me. I went on my own as I have done so very many times for so very many things. It was brilliant. It was life-changing. I would not be writing this book if I hadn't gone.

That five-day workshop challenged me in a million different ways. I met extraordinary people, learned powerful tools and witnessed incredible transformations in others. This kind of stuff is like crack for me. (I can say that because I've done crack.) It blows my mind every time. You bring together a room full of total and complete strangers whose common denominator is they all want something different from what they have. Their willingness and commitment will determine how much they change. In this case, they had all committed to five days of exploration. Like me, no one knew what to expect. All they knew was someone they trusted came in these doors a caterpillar and flew home a butterfly. When you see that kind of metamorphosis, you show up and drink the Kool-Aid.

You can discover more about a person in an hour of play than in a year of conversation.

Plato

As I listened to each of the assistant coaches introduce themselves on Day One of the seminar, I stared at the banner with that quote hanging above the conference room. The coaches invited us to dive in and play hard, and play hard I did. That meant showing up for those five days and for two more weekend workshops, all about different exercises and games to inspire learning and insights. I noticed a common formula in the workshops I'd taken over the years to excavate emotional pain and negative behaviours in order to replace them with positive behaviours. It felt like I was being distracted with something shiny to lower my mental defenses. By keeping my mind occupied, chances were better that I could have a spontaneous reaction rather than a contrived one. My natural reactions offered new observations about myself. Awareness and a willingness to do things differently are the critical first steps to making any major shift in our lives.

Today, I can be transparent with my clients, guiding them to a direct experience of their truth. They have all the answers they need. My job is helping them clear whatever is in the way of their own wisdom.

I first began facilitating change when I volunteered as part of the Choices coaching team. All alumni were invited to come back as small group leaders to support new participants.

The cynics in my life said it was a brilliant business model for free labour. That was one way of looking at it.

I went anyway. I paid my own way, paid for my own accommodations and food. The hours were long, and as volunteers, our breaks were spent in meetings, discussing our small groups. I was physically and emotionally exhausted at the end. Of course, this isn't the kind of work you do for the money. You do it because you love it.

That workshop was life-changing for me and many others as well. We were all willing to do whatever we could to support others to go from pain and suffering to serenity.

Even back then I was coaching. For my whole life I have been coaching. I am a natural cheerleader and problem solver. I can look at someone's story and discern the issue. I can see their strengths and weaknesses and feel intuitively how to support them. That's who I am. Anyone who spent time with me in those workshops would tell you the same. So being there as a teaching assistant was the perfect place for me. Although I remember being exhausted and newly sober back then, burning the candle from all directions, I volunteered twice, and I have the T-shirts to prove it.

The Choices workshops cracked me open and released a lot of pain. They filled me with new ideas and an action plan to live a better life. I was high at the end of every workshop, five days filled with emotional purging and deep connection. As an assistant coach, I was focusing all my energies on supporting the participants in their journey and then celebrating their breakthroughs with them. Whatever the role, at the end of the workshop I was surrounded by so much love and joy that I couldn't help but be affected in the most delightful way.

How do you sustain that level of bliss?

With action.

Teaching what we learned grounded it for ourselves. Whenever you want to remember something, teach it to someone else. That takes it from the one dimension of reading or memorizing to a three-dimensional experience. The more you do it, the closer you get to mastery of whatever you've learned. In recovery we say, "You have to give it away to keep it."

I've Seen Pain From Both Sides Now

The rooms of recovery (Twelve-Step support group meetings) are a magical space where you can be heard without judgement and held with love. Everyone there is well-versed in the art of listening without the need to judge or fix. Well, at least we are all trying to be that way. We all have our own problems and we are all responsible for them. Recovery promotes a powerful lesson of self-responsibility. There is no power in being a victim. When we want to change a situation, we are trained to look at our part in that situation. We talk a lot about being powerless in recovery: being powerless over alcohol and being powerless over other people. The only power we have is to change ourselves and move forward. We all have the same instructions, The Twelve Steps, and yet each of us has a program of recovery unique to our own life circumstances.

A foundational principle in Twelve-Step programs is "a God of my understanding." The Twelve-Step programs are not religious programs; they are spiritual programs built on the premise that since we are powerless over alcohol (or anything we are addicted to), we can't stop drinking, drugging, having sex, gambling etc., on our own. We need a "Higher Power," something outside ourselves to surrender to for help. The brilliance of recovery is that no one tells me what my Higher Power is. I have the sovereignty to choose what my Higher Power is for me and you are free to choose what your Higher Power is for you.

Another key concept in recovery is "Take what you like and leave the rest." I was relieved to see that no one was trying to control or manipulate me. Having that liberty to decide for myself what would work allowed the rebel in me to stand down. I had the ability to create my own program of recovery uniquely suited to my beliefs and background. People shared openly about what worked to help them stay sober and about where they failed. When I first quit drinking, I found amazing solace in the meetings I attended. There was no authority figure pushing their own agenda and that is why, with all my authority issues, I could stick around to listen and learn.

I never wanted to consider that I needed to stop drinking until my life felt so hopeless that I had no other choice. They call it "hitting rock bottom." It took the most incredible misery for me to let my guard down and surrender to a Higher Power for help to stop drinking. Back then I was positive that drinking was the only thing keeping me going. Alcoholism is a twisted disease that has you believing the poison destroying your life is your salvation. I couldn't stop drinking on my own. If I was to escape the madness, I needed a Super Power, a God of my understanding.

Faith in something greater than myself is what makes my life manageable. I heard many times in AA meetings that my sobriety depended on my spiritual condition and now I know my serenity also depends on my spiritual condition. For me, the word "spiritual" means kindness and love. My journey has been about releasing anything in the way of feeling love in order to treat myself and others with kindness. I knew early on that the distress I felt was beyond human help and I had been on a spiritual quest from childhood, gathering information to ease my suffering. Yet while I was in the throes of addiction, I wasn't actively practicing any of the tools I had learned. I realized that in order to live life without alcohol I had to make caring for myself a priority. I had to learn to navigate my intense emotions without alcohol. My addiction had become a life or death situation and it was made clear to me that if I didn't quit drinking, I would destroy myself. What I didn't know was how long my destruction would take and I decided I didn't want to find out.

I was astonished to recognize that recovery teaches spirituality as a process to stop drinking, and discovered the life-saving strength of depending on something greater than myself, my Higher Power, to help me do what I couldn't do alone. I learned The Twelve Steps and began focusing on my spiritual path as a way to to quit drinking, which then became a new way to do everything. For me, that was establishing a connection to a Higher Power through prayer, meditation and continuing my spiritual search until I found Accelerated Evolution. There, I experienced even higher states of consciousness, expanding my capacity for love and kindness.

Today I nurture my spiritual condition as a part of living my life to the fullest, which includes choosing a healthy lifestyle and not drinking. I take great comfort in my belief that there is an infinite energy that cares for all of us. When I come up against impossible questions like why did someone die from addiction, a disaster or Covid and I'm still alive, I cling to my belief that there is a Universal Power that loves all of us and knows all the answers. I comfort myself with the thought that someday I'll know the answers too, just not yet. Over time I have cultivated an acceptance of death as a part of life. I have a deep respect and love for our unique life experience as a conscious being with choice.

Lessons To Ease The Pain

How did I get to this place of acceptance where I enjoy peaceful understanding? A pivotal lesson was living through the painful deterioration and loss of someone I loved, a dear friend who killed herself. She was intelligent, articulate, kind and generous, a very special human in so much emotional pain that her best solution was to take her own life.

She had struggled with staying sober all the years I knew her. She would have a few years sober here or there, then go out drinking and binge for a while until she went to a "detox," an addiction treatment centre, to keep her safe while her body was withdrawing from her alcohol dependency.

She admitted herself to be monitored for withdrawal symptoms. The symptoms from alcohol withdrawal vary from person to person. They can include anxiety, depression, hallucinations, sleeping problems, shakiness—especially in the hands, instability in blood pressure and heart rate, sweating, nausea and vomiting. Extreme cases can include delirium tremens (DTs), a life-threatening issue that can make you restless, upset and confused. They may even cause fever, hallucinations and seizures.

My friend endured many of these in her regular fourteen or thirty-day interments and then the whole cycle started again. Around and around she went until she and everyone who adored her was dizzy.

I loved her deeply. She was brilliant; she'd kick your ass at Scrabble, wielding her knowledge of the English language with the precision of a master yet staying humble and keeping it light. She had brilliant wit and a compelling snort that kept me laughing while I was getting pulverized in the game. She knew so many words I didn't know or hadn't used that she could make me forget English was my first language.

She also worshipped animals. Walking anywhere with her took twice as long as with anyone else, in fact doing anything with her would take longer because she talked to everyone along the way, whether they had four legs or two. When she started a conversation with someone, she was actually listening to their answer only for the sake of hearing their story. She had no agenda; she was truly interested in what people had to say. She often brought people little surprise gifts, which was ridiculous because she was on a fixed income. None of that mattered to her. She was generous on every level. She wasn't working and so she volunteered a lot of her time.

When she wasn't volunteering, she would be helping a friend or learning something new. She was always learning. Sometimes it was Japanese flower arrangement, sometimes it was a new medication for anxiety or manic depression. I've never met anyone quite like her. She had such an honesty and kindness about her that it didn't take much time in her presence for you to fall in love with her.

My heart broke every single time she went back out drinking. One time another friend and I went to visit and found her pissed out of her mind, early in the day, maybe around 10 a.m. We scooped her up, packed her bags and carried her off to my friend's place, determined to have her return to sobriety with us. There we sat with her day and night, waiting for the alcohol to leave her system so we could have our friend back.

After a week it seemed like the light was back in her eyes and she said she felt more grounded. Being that she was an adult and certainly not new to this whole thing, we thought she would be OK, so we let go of our twenty-four hour surveillance, optimistic that she would again stay clean for a while. We were hoping she could stay sober for months, maybe years, God willing, forever.

However, when I saw her the next day, she was drunk. It is the most disturbing, terrifying, heart-wrenching moment when you look into someone's eyes and notice they are not there. The person you love, the person you look up to for their intelligence and kindness. The person who makes you laugh and feel safe. That person is gone. They've been abducted by the spirit of vodka or wine or gin, or whatever drug of choice. All that matters is that the spirit has seduced her and she's lost again. You don't know if she'll ever come back. The crushing truth was revealed to me as I stood in the afternoon sun, leaning over the car to talk to her. It was all in her eyes and in the liquor on her breath.

My heart was in my throat. I felt sick to my stomach from the terror of what would happen to her now. I knew at that moment there was nothing I could do. I had sat with her night and day, pouring my heart and soul, everything I had, into fighting off the alcohol to bring her back to safety. I loved her, nourished her, listened to her and held her. None of it mattered. It was a complete and total waste of time and energy. I turned away from the car and dragged myself back up the sidewalk to my apartment. I was emotionally, physically and spiritually shattered. I was in mourning.

For weeks after, I walked around like someone had died. I went to meetings and I cried. The old-timers in AA, people who had been sober for twenty-plus years, pulled me aside to ask what had happened. When I told them my story, they laid their hands on my shoulder while they listened. The somber look on their faces told me they'd been there. Once I said my piece, they reminded me of the tragic truth I had heard over and over from years of meeting after meeting after meeting. We are alcoholics and no one can save us. No one can stop us from drinking. We have to want to stop drinking for ourselves. We do it or we die.

Of course, I knew it was true, I had known it since the beginning. Over the years I had watched many acquaintances go out drinking again. Hearing someone has gone "back out" feels like a deep loss. It's a brutal reminder of the precarious nature of sobriety. Addiction is a relentless demon, always there waiting for you to screw up and succumb to your old dark ways. In the past, I could always push it all away with a shiver. This time was completely different; this time that truth was playing out in front of me, live and in-person, using someone I loved. I had never felt such intense powerlessness, not even with my own alcoholism. The pain of witnessing her loving being vanish into the anguish of addiction was so sharp I hunched over from the aching in my chest.

That was the last time I ever felt that inconsolable.

A friend told me that the Inuit have over fifty words for snow. They know snow intimately. It is a foundational part of their daily life and their vocabulary naturally reflects that. I looked up the synonyms for pain and found over one hundred. Words like "torment," "harm" and "evil" were on the list. At first I was surprised to see the word "evil." Then I remembered all the abuse and agony my friend had endured. After that, "evil" made perfect sense. Even so, words like "pain" are not enough for people like me. I need magnifiers like "excruciating," "debilitating," "brutal" or "demoralizing."

After what happened with my friend, I was buried under a world of sorrow. I could barely move. It was that way until it wasn't. I don't know how long it took for me to recover but I do know I was never the same as I had been. It's like the first time you love someone and they break your heart or when someone or something like hope dies. You will recover, God willing. Only you are forever changed. Your view of the world is different. The way you love is different. For me, that meant loving her with space to protect myself. I wish I could sound like a more evolved person and say I loved her just the same, only back then that wasn't true.

After my heart was decimated watching my friend get drunk and lose everything she had worked for, I had no other choice but to keep my distance. It was a matter of self-preservation. I was incapable of opening my heart to her in the same way. It felt like it could kill me if I had to go through that again.

Thankfully, over time she got sober once more and we hung out again. Then she "went out" another time after that, and another time and another time and another time. I loved her all through those years. I loved her with my heart behind bulletproof glass. There had to be protection. There was an energetic separation from loving her 100%. There was a numbness that came over me when I talked to my drunk friend, a kind of self-medicating to prevent me from going all in because I never knew what she was going to do.

Until it happened.

It was a Saturday morning just before Christmas when I got the phone call. My friend had killed herself a few days earlier. I did the math in my head and it was the day after we had been for our long-awaited walk that she hung herself in her closet.

What an awful moment. The news itself was not a shock. I knew she was in a lot of trouble with her bipolar disorder and drinking but there had been nothing I could do. In fact, I had physically distanced myself from her for weeks, maybe months. I needed to fortify myself against the alcohol and drug-induced annihilation she was living. I needed time to accept her exactly as she was, to make peace with her living life her way even if it meant watching her destroy herself. I was looking for a way to be strong enough to do that.

I had only just reached out to her for what turned out to be our last walk together, our last hug goodbye. When I heard about her death, I was sorrowful, of course. I was relieved, too, not for me but for her. There was a wave of peace that washed over me when I heard the news because it felt like at last she was free. All her life she had been held hostage by trauma, abuse, mental illness and addiction while she was tossed around like a dirty rag doll until she completely came apart.

At last she was liberated and the wretchedness was over. Witnessing her suffering was a level of heartache I hope never to know again. When I felt the wave of tranquility, it was like her soul was telling my soul she was OK at last. For once and for all, she knew the serenity she had been chasing. When I saw her apartment, it was evident that she had been preparing for her escape. Her place was spotless. When I saw all the envelopes of keys, each precisely labelled with the name of the lock it belonged to, I felt her intentions. Long before the suicide note was found, the message was clear. She was done. She couldn't do it anymore and it was time to stop. Wandering through the rooms where she lived, remembering our dinners together and hearing her laughing while touching her things, I knew her death was meticulously planned and it was her choice. I got it but at the same time I was yearning for a different outcome. It broke my heart and it made perfect sense to me all at the same time.

Staring into the empty corner of the closet, I was confronted with the consequences of living with her haunting, hopeless, terrifying and relentless truth day in and day out. Standing there I let go of my naive wish for a different outcome. How could there be any other conclusion? Facing the space where she took her last breath, feeling the weight of a despair beyond what most people could even imagine, I realized that her choice made sense. She was done suffering, and for that I was grateful.

Ending The Suffering: Your Choice is Your Power

Whatever your mind can conceive and believe, it can achieve.

Napoleon Hill

Believe something different is possible. Believe it and you can achieve it. It can be a spiritual awakening, a voice that speaks to you, more like, whispers the truth to you. You have a "Knowing" inside of you that will lead you in the right direction when you listen. The most powerful moment of hearing my "Knowing" whisper was at my Choices workshop. Choices are the lightsabers that cut through the darkness, leading us into the light. Your "Knowing" will whisper to you at a crucial turning point and show you the right direction. Choosing to follow your "Knowing" cuts through the bullshit with the ease of a hot knife through soft butter. My "Knowing" whispered the question, "What if she's right?"

"She" was Thelma Box, the sixtyish, petite spitfire from Texas running the workshop. Thelma may have been short but there was nothing small about her. She had the emotional strength of a lioness and the confidence of the sun. No one questions the rising and setting of the sun, and no one questioned Thelma. She knew things and she never backed down until you knew them too.

"I want you to quit drinking for the rest of your life." That was her challenge to me.

"No fucking way," was the answer in my head. "No. I can't do that. I can't promise you something I don't know I can do," was my outside voice. For me to "quit drinking for the rest of my life" was an absurd challenge. It hurt my head to contemplate because it was so impossible. I knew immediately that it was beyond the scope of anything I could comprehend. It was like looking at a math problem on your trigonometry test after you've skipped the last three weeks of class and you haven't the slightest clue where to begin and there is no way to fake it so you just throw your hands up in the air.

"No, I am not doing that," was my reply when she kept hounding me. I may have been able to articulate something like, "Are you out of your mind?" Quitting for the rest of my life was a concept completely outside the scope of my mental capacities. It was up there with understanding north, south, east and west. I knew what the words meant, I could point to them on a map, but in day-to-day life, I didn't have a clue how to find them. "That's impossible," I stated with certainty.

I was arguing with her when the "Knowing" whisper happened, like a hairline crack in the dam before all hell breaks loose from the pressure of the water. It may look small, even insignificant in the moment. It's only in retrospect that we can identify that instant as the moment everything changed. Who can fight the power of nature?

That whisper was a shock because although it was coming from inside me, it wasn't my voice and it wasn't a thought. I knew it was real and wasn't imagined. It was powerful. It had shocked me and captured my attention, nullifying all of my arguments.

"What if she's right?" I remember looking around to see who was speaking, knowing it most certainly was not me. And who else could it be with such peace and authority? Such clarity and non-judgement? It must be God speaking.

That was my Spiritual Awakening.

I was standing at the crossroads: Yes, I will quit drinking, or No, I will not quit drinking. Once upon a time more people would have thought I was nuts for saying something like "God spoke to me." Maybe there are people who consider the idea of "hearing voices" as something that only happens as a consequence of mental illness rather than being open to the idea that it can also happen when you connect to your Higher Self. What I am saying is that I am grateful to notice that more and more people understand the concept of God or your

Higher Self speaking to you. It's a voice you hear from inside you, somewhere that is not a part of your body. You hear a voice but it's not from your mind.

That whisper destroyed my argument, taking my legs out from under me like the whoosh of a wave when your back's to the ocean. It cancelled any question in my mind. Still, being the rebel I was, I spoke up with my own conditions. I'll quit drinking and go to meetings three days a week for three months. That's it. That's the best I can promise. I needed something I was convinced I could accomplish. I remember thinking that it would be easier to stop breathing than to stop drinking for the rest of my life. Looking back, the choice to quit drinking for three months was the first in a long line of conscious choices that saved my life. The first choice to end my addiction to alcohol was literally a life-saving choice while the rest have been life-enhancing choices. They have all been either soul-saving, sanity-saving, serenity-maintaining, suffering-depleting, freedom-grounding, beautiful life-affirming or life-improving choices.

The first power of choice is the power of making a decision. When I was actively addicted to alcohol, my life was a wreck. I was searching to understand why my life was a wreck, which for me was a lot of time and energy contemplating my situation, while I continued to suffer. The agony and destruction of my addiction did not end until I made a choice between drinking and not drinking. Moving from confusion about my situation to choosing a plan of action shifted my energy and empowered me to move forward.

The second power of choice is the power of perspective. Whatever happens to me in life, I can choose how I look at it, how I think about it and what I believe about it. I am the only one who can choose my outlook, and how I see things changes my experience of them. One step at a time, my choices carry me forward toward my truth. They come in all sizes, from seemingly insignificant to life-changing. The size of the choice doesn't matter. It's living the practice day in and day out that matters. Realizing that I had the power to consciously choose my thoughts, which become feelings that impact my behaviour, was a game-changer for me.

This saying comes to mind:

How you do anything is how you do everything.

T. Harv Eker

Whether it is choosing how I react to spilling matcha all over the counter in the morning or choosing to quit drinking or not to quit drinking, it is the conscious act of deciding and noticing how the choice I make impacts my experience. When I spill my matcha these days, I am conscious of my thoughts and how they dictate what kind of morning I'm in for. A thought like, "What an idiot! I can't believe I did that!" can run through my mind, and it's up to me whether I focus on that thought or focus instead on something like, "OMG! You're hilarious, Smith. Slow down." I choose which I focus on and notice the feelings like anger and frustration or silliness and acceptance that come up.

My choice to say, "Yes, I will quit drinking," was the first and most special choice of many in a powerful journey. I make that choice every single day. Every day I choose not to drink, I choose peace over chaos and my wellbeing over my self-destruction. That daily action of choosing me and my happiness fills me with the power to make other choices that feed me. I choose a daily practice that may look like writing in the morning, meditating, bouncing on my rebounder, dancing in my office, practicing yoga, whatever supports me best that day. I choose what to eat. I choose how much sleep I get and who my friends are. I choose how I think about everything from myself to the Covid virus. My thoughts are the colours with which I paint my world.

Extremes are easy for me to understand and illustrate the contrast of my thinking and my experience. I am worthless or I am powerful. I am beautiful or I am ugly. I can do it or I can't do it. I love myself or I hate myself. He loves me or he doesn't love me.

When I think something like, "I am worthless," it sends my brain, the most incredible computer processor, on a mission to find evidence to support my thought. I start reflecting on the experiences of my life through the context of "me being worthless" and I find episodes and instances of my actions proving that I am worthless. It is a self-fulfilling prophecy.

That thought shapes how I feel in my body. When I think, "I am worthless," my energy drops. Even the light changes in my mind and the world becomes a dark place. My posture changes, and I hang my head and slump my shoulders. I don't want to go out in the world. Maybe I don't even get out of my bed. When I think, "I am worthless," I believe everyone else thinks it too. So even when people say or do kind things, I don't believe them. I can't accept them. It is a painful place to be. My own prison cell, created in my own mind.

Impenetrable.

When I think, "I am beautiful," I feel a smile in my heart and on my face. There is light in me and around me. My body feels open and powerful. I have the confidence to go out and enjoy the world. I see other beautiful people and things. I take pleasure in the good I see and feel. When people say or do kind things for me, I am able to let them in.

The Power of Choice reigns over everything: my thoughts, my words, my actions. I can choose love or I can choose fear. Every choice I make begins a chain reaction of thought, feeling, action. If someone says something unkind to me, I can choose a thought like, "They must be having a bad day," or "Maybe I misunderstood," and with that choice, remain in the state of bliss that I'm experiencing. That feeling informs the action I take. I can choose to say something kind back to them or ask them a question from a neutral place and retain my state of peace. Choosing my thoughts creates my feelings, my behaviours, my circumstances and ultimately my reality.

That is true power.

The Gifts That Come When You Stop Poisoning Yourself

I've talked about my first AA meeting where I heard a woman talking about her fear of never being able to have fun without alcohol. She also talked about making friends in recovery and about the belly laughs they shared. Up until I heard her story about making friends and having fun, I didn't believe that was possible. It was a fundamental relief to know there was a different way of living

I saw other people living the life I wanted. They were proof it was possible and that fuelled my desire to keep going. I saw people cracking jokes and throwing potluck dinners and laughing with lifelong friends. I wanted that. I would have done anything to have that connection, belonging and joy.

I would tell the truth about every wretched thing I had ever done. I would relive it and write down all the people I had hurt and how I hurt them. I would write about the endless ways I tried to destroy myself. I would let it all out of my body. The surprise is that I would learn to accept myself for everything I had done. I would dig my way out of the putrid hatred that had buried me alive. I would climb out and take a hot shower in forgiveness to wash it all away. And it never, never came back.

That's the power of The Twelve Steps. It was a road map to salvation. A gift from all those who went before me. Over coffee and donuts, they told me what to do and I was willing to do the work. They showed me how and, miracle of miracles, I was on the path to happy destiny.

I don't talk a lot about those dark days anymore. It was long ago and far away. The people who love me now know, without a lot of details, I had hard times. They don't care about those details. They love the me in front of them today, no matter what details they learn about my past. That's the unimaginable gift when you accept yourself. You attract people to love and accept you as you are. No questions. No judgements. If you want to talk about it, cool, if you don't, that's groovy too.

As I write this now, I look back and I see there were always people willing to love and accept me even when I felt the most repulsive. In my mind, I was a big bag of puss walking around, just waiting to explode. My self-image was fixated on my emotional ugliness. Think of words like sludge, putrid, disgusting, gruesome, grotesque, dark, twisted, broken... So many words to describe what was wrong with me. That's what I saw and how I thought about myself.

Thank God there were people who saw the light in me shining through all the shame, hatred and humiliation. They saw me bright and beautiful when I felt like I was a disgusting pile of garbage covered in filth I couldn't wash clean. They knew none of that was true. They saw me before I even knew who I was. I tell this story now in case you don't know that you are the most precious soul. You are beauty and power beyond words. Now, I am the one seeing you there, a pure being surrounded by unconditional love. All the shame and hatred are just stories that keep you from the miraculous truth of who you are. You are love. You are loved. It is already true. Everything else is a lie, it's not real. I know it's not real because I've lived in nightmares and self-hatred, feeling like a pile of maggots was eating me from the inside. Thank God, I realized it was a nightmare of my own creation, which meant that since I had the power to make it up, I had the power to let it go.

Our life is made up of the stories we tell ourselves. At last, I've made friends with the Boogeyman, that part of me born from the pain and ugliness I experienced. In my journey to escape the clutches of this monster living in the dark side of my soul, I was amazed to discover that even this grotesque being that I used to run from ultimately had my highest good at heart. Once I had the courage to look at this part of me, to feel the terrifying emotions, I understood that they had powerful messages for me.

What if everything that has happened to you has happened for your awakening? For most of my life, looking for the good in each situation has given me great comfort with anything difficult I experienced, except what happened to my mom. I am a natural optimist and recognizing the advantages in getting fired or my boyfriend breaking up with me was normal. However, it never occurred to me to apply this perspective to that terrifying night from my childhood. That incident seemed to be too horrible for me to attempt to look for the good in it. Only when a coach prompted me to ask the question, "What's good about it?" did I find the key for unlocking the door to my ultimate freedom from the pain of the past.

Reach out your hand and let me guide you out of the clutches of your nightmares to the freedom, joy and peace that await you.

Trauma

Trauma:
1a: an injury (such as a wound) to living tissue caused by an
extrinsic agent
b: a disordered psychic or behavioural state resulting from severe
mental or emotional stress or physical injury
c: an emotional upset

2: an agent, force, or mechanism that causes trauma

Merriam-Webster Dictionary

Throughout my life, I received messages to minimize my issues. "It's not that big a deal," people would say. I felt like I was programmed to push things down and act like I was OK immediately after any life-impacting incident. A perfect example of this many can relate to is a car accident. The immediate response you hear from people is, "I'm OK," even when they often don't know if they are OK. We need time to evaluate the impact on our body. I know I did when I was in that car accident.

Trauma can be a scary word. The term brings up the possibility of unspeakable tragedy, incredible pain and suffering, and out-of-control emotional outbursts. Generally, people are uncomfortable with all of these. There is the unspoken idea that it is next to impossible to recover from trauma. People are reluctant to use the word, especially when talking about themselves. It's much easier to avoid dealing with something when it "wasn't that big a deal."

I have decided that I will stop using the word "trauma." I want all of us to be free from that label. Choosing a different word relaxes our opposition to addressing the effects of our painful past. Using a different term frees people to explore the impact of any difficult incident. What happened is less important than how it affects you now. I've decided that in this book I'll be using words like "intense experience," "adversity" or "painful past." None of these has the stigma or power of the T word. For me, the turning point in overcoming an intense experience was realizing that it wasn't what happened to me that was causing my suffering. That was over and gone, just one moment in time. The misery was in all the unconscious emotions and beliefs I held onto around my experience. The issue: what I thought about what had happened. The miracle came from recognizing that we all have the capacity to change the way we think about our experiences.

What I've witnessed with myself and my clients is that if something shocking has happened and has left you feeling powerless, and that intense event is still adversely affecting your life today, the way to freedom *from* it is *through* it. For me, it was all about accepting the past rather than running away from it. I knew that I needed help and that addressing my history with the support of a professional would alleviate my suffering.

Another thing I've learned about sharing my past is that, although the details of what happened are different for everyone, the consequences are surprisingly similar. We can't change what happened in the past. The good news is that we can change how we think and feel about the past. It's all about coming into the present and taking our power back from what happened so that we live our lives in this moment. The magic happens in the here and now.

I have always been someone open to self-discovery and personal development on a conscious level. However, on an unconscious level, there were many issues my higher self was hiding from me until I was ready to address them. Timing is everything. Through my life, I found that the stronger I became and the better support I connected with, the more challenging issues I discovered. It still surprises me that while searching for my purpose at age fifty, I discovered that an intense childhood experience needed more attention.

It may sound strange for me to say that it was a surprise; however,

I believe it speaks to the whole movement towards minimizing our challenges. Before that moment of realization, I had been confident that I had dealt with the intense event. I had done counselling, workshops, and the work from AA's Twelve-Step program. I even had endless pages of journalling that explored my feelings about what happened. How could it possibly be the case that this childhood event was still a cause of my misery?"

I heard messages from society telling me to minimize what happened. Lord knows my family was on board with that. "Keep your problems to yourself. Never, and I mean never, confide any issues with an outsider." I was told that I should keep my problems in the home. In my European household, I felt like there was an "us and them" mentality. This was not malicious but rather a survival principle. Whatever happens inside stays with us. Show them, the outside world, your best face. A common North American expression about this belief system is, "Everything is OK, nothing to see here."

That was exhausting.

For many years I didn't have a conscious awareness of this unspoken training, I simply went along with it. I am not blaming anyone, or judging them. I am only making an observation. My family is no different from countless other families. I'll take responsibility for my part, which was continuing to act in an unconscious manner. Certainly, it is possible that I misunderstood or misinterpreted what was meant. Maybe if I had gone to an adult to tell them what happened with my mother sooner than I did, they would have taken me to the authorities. I don't know because that's not what I did at the time. To this day, I have no clue if my mom realized I was there when it happened.

It has been suggested to me that I waited to write this book until my mother passed away because it wasn't only my story to tell. The main character in this drama was indeed my mother. It is only because of this book that I confided in my dad about what happened. Until then, he had no idea. My dad was working out of town when it happened and there was no disclosure at the time. After my disclosure, he did recall my mother sharing a secret with him about being assaulted, years after the fact. Looking back, he recognized that the timing she gave him would have fit for this story.

As you can imagine, it was an intense conversation when I told my dad. I had been contemplating what to say for weeks. What could possibly be the reason to dig up such a harrowing secret? Especially when the secret could just as easily stay buried with my mother. Why on earth would I open the door to the possible agony that could arise for him from sharing my story, something so private, in such a public way as a book? Because

Our secrets keep us sick.

The darker the secrets, the sicker you become. The things you are afraid of, all the things that you bury, hoping for time to decompose and disintegrate rather than dealing with them yourself, these are the things that hold you hostage. The most terrifying, cruel, blood-curdling events are the gatekeepers of your freedom, and the truth will set you free. That's not a cliché. It's real. I know because I have been there.

I understand that denial is a coping mechanism, and I also recall that coping sucks. Being in a state of chronic coping is like having a leech on steroids bonded to your soul. It slowly but surely will drain every single, precious drop of life out of you. I wasn't going to let that happen to me. I wanted freedom from the past.

My mother and I are free of the shame, anger and pain. I believe it wasn't until her death that my mom disengaged from all her torment. Thankfully, death wasn't the only way for me to break free of what had been holding me back. I've searched, studied and practiced other ways, and today I am free too.

When I was ready for liberation, I found the perfect coach for me, Angela, who introduced me to a new modality called Accelerated Evolution. I didn't do it alone. I was willing to see things differently and had the courage to go down that ugly memory lane and live it one last time to find a way out of hell. It takes love and it takes trust. I believed that freedom from a lifetime of slavery created by that one moment was worth feeling the pain in a controlled environment. Angela was a safe, loving guide with the energetic depth and strength to keep me from getting lost in the pain of the experience. I went into that dark place over a few sessions until the miracle happened; my mind and body released the vise grip on the emotions around the memory. Thanks to my belief that better was possible, along with the sagacious guidance of my coach, I was able to feel my whole being let go.

The memory of the event was still there. It happened, and nothing can change that. The magic was that I no longer suffered the pain, shame, anger or fear around that experience. I wasn't shut down any longer. My body was instead filled with space and light. For the first time in my life I had a different story and I felt like myself. I tell myself that new story every day. I am a brilliant being because of all the choices I've made since what happened. I decide how my past affects me and I choose to be powerful.

Thank you, Universe!

I am free at last!

In my storytelling, I delve into that experience over and over, and I am grateful to say that no matter how much I talk about it, the emotions have never come back. My relief is profound and sustainable. I am always open about what happened to my mother, about my addiction, and about any other difficulties from my past and how they impacted me. Whenever I listen to someone else who is suffering from the impact of intense violation, I can hold the space for them to be vulnerable, sharing my knowing, my inner certainty, that they did nothing wrong. It is a bizarre truth that as victims we often blame ourselves for what happened. I certainly did.

I remember torturing myself after an incident with a bully in elementary school. Oh, the many fantasies about me stopping the attack from happening. That's so much more attractive than the powerless feeling after being slapped around, unable to protect myself from the older giant of a student. As a child I mistakenly took responsibility for what happened. It was the same with my mother's assault. Over the following decades I punished myself and subconsciously felt I was bad because I hadn't stopped what happened. With the work I've done, I no longer feel shame about what took place.

The sooner you can let go of any misguided and misplaced shame, the sooner you will be free of the shackles of what happened and ready to live an extraordinary life.

Puppet Strings Of The Past

Lack Of Confidence

Clients often say to me, "I want more confidence." Why? Because the confident people get the sales, the attention, the good parking spaces... I remember back when I was not feeling very confident, I couldn't help but notice the very confident people around me. They jumped out at me. I watched them with a sense of wonder and admiration, mesmerized by how they worked the room at an event or by their social media presence. Now that I feel confident, it seems like I walk taller; the weight that was pushing me down has been lifted and talking to people is a lot easier.

I invite you to try something with me. Are you sitting in a quiet place without distraction? Sit back in your chair with your back straight, close your eyes and take a few deep breaths. Inhale through your nose, exhale out your mouth. Breathe into this present moment, exhaling and letting go of everything that came before. Relax into your body and feel your feet on the ground. Now, I want you to feel confident. Think about a specific time when you felt confident, and go there in your imagination as if it were happening right now. See what you saw then, hear what you heard then, experience what you were experiencing then. Take a few moments and remember the images you saw, the thoughts you heard in your head, feel the emotions that arise, and the body sensations you felt at the time.

When you're ready, open your eyes.

How do you feel now? You've just changed your feelings by choosing different thoughts. I do guided visualizations like this with my clients. Anytime you want to feel more confident, you can do an exercise like this for yourself.

Before I had my epiphany about my mother's ordeal, I didn't

realize that the shock of that event had locked a lot of my confidence away in a secret vault. For so many years, all my gifts and talents were a painful mystery to me. They were hidden from me like needles in a haystack. My whole life was spent looking for them. This was a conundrum to people I worked with and to my husband most of all. They thought my skills and talents were obvious. It didn't make sense that I didn't know what my gifts and talents were when I was using them on a regular basis. In fact, my husband would get frustrated with me when I couldn't see what was right in front of my nose.

Back then I felt a pain in my chest like something was pushing down on me whenever I would ask myself the hard question: "What am I good at?" I could feel something physically blocking me from knowing the answer. Now I realize the intense childhood experience had seriously warped my self-image. Back then, nothing made sense and there was a lingering feeling that no one could be trusted, including me. Looking back, I realize that all the years of thinking things like, "I wasn't able to stop what happened to my mom, so what good am I?" had created the belief that I was a loser, inadequate to the nth degree. Any time I thought I could escape this fate, the history rose up, obscured in the dark robe of the cruellest overlord, and I was banished back to the depths of the cave where I shrunk in the darkness reserved for the pathetic person I was. All I needed were a few key words like, "Who do you think you are? You'll never amount to anything," or my personal favourite, "You're a piece of shit," to remind me where I belonged.

If I had a friend experiencing all these symptoms and I knew what had happened to them, I would be saying, "Look at what happened to you as a kid! Of course, you will be feeling this way." Only when it was happening to me, my history felt so normal. I was used to minimizing it with thoughts like: "It wasn't a big deal." "No need to dredge up the past. It doesn't matter anymore." "Other people have been through much worse." And so on…

Lack Of Fun

Drinking was a magical solution for me. I was bolder, stronger and way more fun when I was loaded. Alcohol was a gift to me with its carefree attitude which was a godsend after years of worry and obsession. Alcohol allowed me to relax and let go of that feeling of having my back up to the wall all the time.

Once the alcohol was gone, so was my easy recipe for fun. I was back to being the uptight control freak who couldn't relax. It was never more obvious than when I was with my husband. He is a jokester. He is light-hearted, fun and has a life purpose to make people laugh. That is why I married him. (Well, that and he's gorgeous, and very sexy.) I love that he's easygoing and always has a humorous outlook. Only I rarely laughed at his jokes. This was a bone of contention in our marriage and it is only recently that I had the insight that this inability to laugh at his jokes had also stemmed from what happened to my mother. It wasn't safe to relax and laugh at jokes. Relaxing was letting go of control and letting go of control wasn't safe.

Somewhere inside me, there was always the voice screaming, "There will be no relaxing! That could lead to serious danger like being violated by your friend." Oh no. My brain was having none of that. So fun? Nope. That was off the table.

Lack Of Intimacy

Years ago I first heard the definition of intimacy as **in - to - me - see**. I liked that, it made sense, it was clear. With all that had gone on in my life, everything I had inside of me, there was no way in hell I was letting anyone inside. I had determined I was absolutely unlovable. There were many layers of this self-hatred and unworthiness that I released over the years.

The unworthiness could pop up at any time. In fact, I remember a networking meeting where a client was proclaiming a list of accolades for me and my work as a virtual assistant. I was going into a panic attack and listing off in my head all the things I should have been doing better for them. Anytime anyone said anything kind to me, I immediately threw it to the curb. I was convinced they had no idea what they were saying. They didn't have a clue of who I was because if they did, they would most certainly have nothing nice to say to me. In fact, they wouldn't be talking to me in the first place.

This belief system created obstacles in my love life that seemed insurmountable to me. There was plenty of drama and the necessity to control the men around me. I was the beautiful doll you couldn't see rotting on the inside, until you got too close where you could gag from the stench. I carefully chose men who were emotionally in worse shape than me. If they were in better shape emotionally, I told myself they must feel like they were dating a beautiful crazy person.

In my friendships, I used to have an intense need to please, like any good codependent. There was a lot of desperate chasing what I thought I wanted, followed by "screw you" when I didn't get it.

Lack Of Serenity

From childhood, I had been overrun with anxiety. In my early twenties, I took a marketing course with a communication component that included public speaking. I was pretty adept at writing the speeches but when it came to standing in front of everyone, I was sick and terrified. I would be shaking so hard that the rattling of the paper in my hand made it hard to hear what I was saying. It was torture for me.

It was a bizarre experience to go against my instincts like that. On the one hand, I had a job to do; my logical mind was moving me through the steps to read my speech. On the other hand, my survival instincts were freaking me out with feelings of extreme repulsion and terror.

What I didn't realize at the time was this wasn't just the average fear of public speaking, the ancestral fear of speaking in front of the tribe that lives in all of us. In the time when we lived in tribes and everything was about survival, the rules were clear and absolute. There was only one leader and you did what they said; everyone else was a listener and a follower. Otherwise, there would be chaos. The only time you spoke in front of the group was to defend yourself from being banished from the tribe. That was literally a life and death situation because you could die if you were cast out and forced to survive without the tribe.

My deep anxiety came from this universal fear but was also connected to the deep-seated fear of being seen.

That night when my mom was being assaulted, intense shock struck me when I realized what was happening. Then the internal alarm of mortal danger in that moment—"What if he sees me?"—was imprinted in my subconscious. I never understood the deep roots of it until recently. I hated people looking at me. I am an attractive woman but for most of my life, I had been extremely shy and couldn't cope with people noticing me in any way. The juxtaposition of wanting to be invisible and being passionately argumentative resulted in ongoing torment for me. It wasn't until I made a concerted effort to get over this that things changed.

Lack Of Self-Control

I wanted to get past that overwhelming anxiety, which meant doing something about it. In the work I do with clients now, I would call this "paradoxical intention." You take the thing you are scared of and do it over and over until it doesn't scare you anymore. It sounds counterintuitive, I know, but it works amazingly well. One of my solutions for getting over people looking at me was to get a job in a casino dealing blackjack. The fact that I loved playing blackjack could get me through the terror of standing in front of people, plus, I would get paid to do it.

I had been playing cards all my life so the idea of gambling was in my blood. As soon as I was of legal age, my aunt took me to the casino. The adrenaline rush I experienced from playing cards with a limitless opportunity to win money awoke the addict in me and I started gambling hard. Another unexpected payoff from going to the casino was the freedom to be out in public as a single woman having fun on my own terms, without the negative attention I encountered from men when I went to the bar.

In the beginning, I enjoyed playing blackjack because I could be social and relax. There is a camaraderie that can happen between the players when the table is going well and everyone is winning. There was no alcohol in the casinos at the time. The only drug was the adrenaline that came with the rush when I was making all the right decisions and winning more and more money.

Many times I would play the anchor position on the table. This is the last player position before the dealer takes their cards. The decisions I made there directly affected the table because if I could cause the dealer to "bust" (their hand was more than twenty-one), the whole table won their bets. I felt powerful. Of course, if I made the wrong decision and the dealer's hand was twenty-one or blackjack, then everyone lost. For that reason, many people are afraid to play the anchor on the table. It can be a lot of pressure since people are not afraid to share their opinions of your performance.

I remember being uncomfortable too, but I would suck it up and sit in the power position anyway. No doubt it surprised more than one person to see a nineteen-year-old girl with the courage or stupidity to take on the responsibility of playing in that spot. For me, it added to the excitement of the evening.

I was always taught to play as a table, all for one and one for all. If everyone played by the same rules—for example, staying on a hard sixteen to leave cards to make the dealer go bust—then the table had a higher chance of winning. I learned early on that there is a cycle to gambling. When you are winning, there is a limited time until you start the losing part of the cycle. The losing will eventually give way to winning again, only there is absolutely no way to tell when the winning will start. The goal is always to leave "up" or in the winning cycle with more money in your pocket than when you started.

There were nights when I left while I was winning, and those were happy times for me. More often than not, I would hit the losing cycle at the beginning of the evening, before I had any time to enjoy the rush of winning. I would be seduced into pulling out more cash to chase the money I had lost, always telling myself I would win it back. Sometimes I would be on a winning streak and so high from the excitement and success that I wasn't conscious of, or I was in denial of, the slide into the losing cycle. Eventually, in my obsession to win back what I had lost, I would lose all the money I had. Still desperate to drag myself out of the financial pit I was in, I would take a cab home to get more money. Then I would go back to the casino and lose that too.

Sometimes I lost all the money I had plus my mom's money. I was living with my parents at the time but I never asked to borrow her money. I just took it on impulse as part of my intense compulsion to regain my money and the peace of mind I lost with it. Gambling goes in cycles like that. You win, you lose, you win, you lose…

Losing my own money was never fun; however, it wasn't the same as the soul-sucking experience of stealing my mother's money and losing that too. My God, I hated myself when I did that. I knew it was wrong. I would never even consider taking someone's money without asking in any other circumstance but when I was gambling, I was swallowed in a mania with only one focus: to get my money back. Nothing else mattered, or even occurred to me. Everytime I took Mom's money I reassured myself I would pay it back. There were times when I won enough to pay it back the same night. Unfortunately, there were more gut-wrenching nights when I couldn't repay her. Instead, I would be steeped in the shame of what I had done and have to work to reimburse her over time. Whatever plans she had for her money were destroyed by my selfishness.

You would think the guilt, shame and self-hatred would be enough to compel me to assert some self-control and avoid that desperate chase after the stolen money. The problem was I knew the win/lose/win cycles existed and I was frantic to refill the sickening hole in my gut. Only I never knew how much money I would need to pour into the vicious cycle to get back to the winning phase.

When you win, there you are again, on top of the world—you've won your money back and more. Do you walk away?

If you're not addicted to gambling, you probably don't understand the question.

"Of course you walk away!" is your answer.

As a recovering addict myself, I know that when addiction takes hold, I am in the throes of a natural chemical high. Walking away is no simple thing.

According to The Responsible Gambling Council:
When you gamble, your brain releases dopamine, the feel-good neurotransmitter that makes you feel excited. You'd expect to only feel excited when you win, but your body produces this neurological response even when you lose. This means that once the thrill of the moment takes over, some people have trouble recognizing when it is time to stop playing.

So you ride the roller coaster up and down. Up is the high of euphoria and down is the darkest self-loathing. Money is the fuel for this dangerous thrill ride. If you go home a loser, nauseous, with a head full of bitter recriminations tormenting you through a sleepless night, you experience hell.

There were definitely nights when that happened for me. There were nights when I was so high from the rush of getting the money back that I could not pull myself away and lost it all again and even more... Oh my God, the tossing and turning in bed, crying and hating myself. The damning disbelief I had done it again. The rage at being so irresponsible. How was I going to get out of this?

Three jobs, that's how. I started working those jobs with a plan to save my money and travel to Spain. However, once I started gambling, I needed all that extra income to support my reckless habit. I worked the front desk at two hotels and a graveyard shift at a 7-Eleven convenience store. At that time, a woman could work graveyards, 11 p.m. to 7 a.m., alone. The whole thing seemed perfectly natural to me. I knew what I wanted and I was determined to make it happen, despite my parents' horror at the idea of me working graveyards alone.

I often worked sixteen-hour days, and since the hotels were close to the convenience store, occasionally I could manage back-to-back shifts. I was in this wicked gambling nightmare for a year. When I wasn't working, all I wanted to do was go to the casino. I kept telling myself that I worked so hard, I deserved a little fun. I gave up asking any friends to do stuff with me because we were on different schedules. Honestly, I didn't want to do anything else anyway. At the casino I was free to be whoever I wanted. No one ever asked me what I was doing there. I didn't need to explain myself to anyone. There was no past or future. All that mattered was what happened at the table.

Abstinence solved my problem. I needed a job to pay my bills so I gave in to following the rules and became a blackjack dealer at the casino I used to frequent. The addictive gambling came to an abrupt halt. The company had a clear policy restricting employees from gambling in their casinos. Thus ended my gambling.

Need For A Hug

I had a lot of anxiety around men. I was uncomfortable in their presence and I know now it was fear. I had walls around myself and chose to see them as non-sexual beings as much as possible. That meant a lot of talking and focusing on the task at hand. It didn't leave any room for joking around or flirting. To me, sexual tension was dangerous and unbearable. It freaked me out. I didn't understand it. I wanted to stay in control and would always bring things back to discussions and the intellectual perspective where I was comfortable. Basically, I was stuck in the mind of a twelve-year-old girl walking around in a woman's body. I remember times I innocently looked up and noticed a man staring at me, seeing in his eyes something to be very afraid of. I felt like a deer about to be devoured. That feeling of being hunted gave me the heebie-jeebies, so I ran away from it. Sometimes I was running in my mind, ignoring it until it went away, and other times I was physically running away.

One of the stories I told myself was that no one was attracted to me. When I did find someone I was attracted to, and who astonishingly turned out to be attracted to me as well, the sex happened quickly and exactly the way I wanted. My communication skills around sex were awkward in their directness. I would blurt out, "I'm not having sex with you," when that was the case or, "Let's have sex." when that was the case. My demeanour was rigid rather than romantic or playful. No one was going to mistakenly think I wanted them to fuck me. Thankfully a lot of this has changed since then. Reclaiming the playful side of me is an ongoing practice.

When I was first dating my husband, in that time of blissful passion and attraction, I felt aroused just sitting beside him. It was the most bizarre contrast to enjoy the butterflies of new love and still be racked with anxiety stemming from my survival instincts. I was more aware of myself and my feelings in our relationship than with any other man I had dated because with him I was never under the influence of alcohol. My head was full of the insights and learnings from my journey of self-discovery while my body had completely contrary reactions. I was enjoying all the physical arousal and trust for the kindest man I'd ever dated, and at the same time I was confounded by uncontrollable shaking spurts, almost a seizure-like experience when he would come to embrace me.

I see now it was the deep-seated fear stuck in my body that shook me violently like the washing machine when the towels get stuck on one side. The anxiety spread through me like wildfire through dry grass. The closer I got, the more intense the trembling. I was powerless over it. No amount of thinking or logic could ease the involuntary convulsions. Rob may have been the man of my dreams, even so there was still a part of me certain I was on the way to my own death or worse. The only solution we found was to have him hug me hard to calm my nervous system. The tremors decreased over a few weeks because of the hugging and disappeared once we consummated our relationship.

My experience of the healing power of hugging reminds me of the biographical movie, *Temple Grandin*. It's the story of an autistic woman who becomes one of the top scientists in the humane livestock-handling industry. Grandin suffered from extreme anxiety until she stumbled upon a solution on a cattle farm, of all places. Going from her home in the city to visit family in the country, she witnessed cattle calmed by being squeezed. This was a regular practice on the family farm. Fascinated by the effectiveness of the process for cows, she created a contraption to squeeze herself and give herself comfort when in excruciating anxiety. Grandin went on to fight her way through the male-dominated cattle industry to be heard as the expert in the humane treatment of livestock. Just as Grandin's unusual self-hug eased her anxiety, Rob's hugs eased mine.

Commitment, Courage & Coaching

What does it take to free yourself and live your dreams? For me, it took knowing my dream and having the commitment, courage and coaching to make it happen. In the beginning my dream was simple: I wanted to feel better.

Commitment

Commitment was key because at the start, doing the work to feel better seemed like hard labour. I only had the perseverance to focus my efforts in small spurts and there are many levels of commitment. The overall commitment to your goal to transform your life is the big one. It's your commitment to all the steps along the path that carry you to your goal. For some people, that may sound too big. I remember those days when I was so afraid of disappointment that I refused to set any goals. The fear of the torment from disappointment was a wall that would stop me dead in my tracks. It could take weeks, months, even years to get back on the horse. I've learned that it is the reaching for something remarkable that moves us forward.

Shoot for the moon. Even if you miss, you'll land among the stars.

Norman Vincent Peale

However, what trips so many of us up is the daily commitment inside the big picture commitment. It's the daily commitment to the small actions and continuing to have faith, no matter what resistance comes up. Resistance can be strong and obvious, showing up in the form of procrastination. Or it can be less obvious like an uncomfortable feeling, maybe a pain in your chest. I used to think of resistance as an obstacle. These days, I think of resistance as a messenger. What if resistance is a part of you wanting to tell you something? I listen to see what I might be trying to tell myself. The choice I make today is to see my feelings as my allies. Whatever resistance arises, persistence is your saving grace.

One day at a time, or in this case, one action at a time, is simple. Simple is not easy but it is absolutely, 100% achievable. It's just not easy. The commitment is one day at a time, even one hour or one minute at a time. There will be days where you give in to the resistance. That is human nature. That's where the compassion for yourself will soften the blow of a minor setback and keep you on track. **Keep Going.**

Every moment is a new opportunity to start again. The magic of that is light and good and loving and possible. You can make a mistake and still make it back to your daily steps. Experience has taught me that. I learned Transcendental Meditation when I was nineteen years old. It was quite the journey to establish a daily routine. At the outset, I would practice for a few months, then miss a day. The judgement and berating I administered to myself would shut down my routine for months, sometimes even years. I was always looking for some new type of meditation with the unconscious idea that a different type would make it easier for me to set up a daily routine. Of course, it wasn't the type of meditation that was the problem, it was my approach.

I remember maybe seven years ago practicing Transcendental Meditation and having the realization that I would always meditate. It no longer mattered if I missed a day or a week or even a month. I knew that I would always come back to it because it nourished me. Nowadays, more often than not, I meditate in the morning. I still move between different kinds of meditation: guided visualizations, heart rhythm meditation, sitting in silence, breathing, lying on the rug listening to music, looking out the window, walking in the forest, or my newest adventure—Harmonizing Meditation incorporating movement, breathing and the infinity symbol. There is no right or wrong way to meditate. I accept where I am in this moment and do what's in front of me. Letting go of the judgement has given me a daily routine that works for me.

The most powerful commitment of my life is to not drink alcohol. That is a huge transformational commitment, and the only way it works for me is if I break it down into manageable pieces. I take it one day at a time.

When I started the AA program, the slogan "One day at a time" infuriated, bewildered and at times belittled me. I finally came to comprehend the wisdom of this simple concept: it is an instruction, a direction, a touchstone. It's the tried and true answer, time and again, to the question, "How can I do this?"

We can do anything one minute at a time. That leads to the next minute to the next hour to the next day. It can be painful, it can feel excruciating or impossible. Every time you make it through one day, you are a success. You build your strength, your tolerance, faith and know-how. Whatever your "it" (get out of bed after your husband died, speak up for yourself when you are being bullied, trust a new man when you've been lied to or worse), the more you do "it," the more evidence you have for yourself and your brain that "it" is possible. Your rational mind loves evidence.

That's what lets you keep committing.

Courage

Courage is required whenever you enter new territory. Your mind and body are easily freaked out by anything new. Their job is to keep you safe; the unknown, by definition, is not safe. Accept that as your baseline and things become more manageable. I used to be afraid almost all the time. Certainly any time I tried something new my anxiety would flare up. I thought there was something wrong with me. Once I understood that I wasn't doing anything wrong, that my body was doing its job to protect me by freaking out, it became easier to be courageous. After all I'd been through, my body had a long list of things to protect me from. Not to mention all that fear and anxiety that comes from our survival instincts, the part of us that assesses everything in terms of life and death. However, very few things we are afraid of will kill us. Every time you do "it" and don't die, it's proof that "it" is OK.

For me, courage is a lot of deep breaths. What some would call courage has, at times, felt like desperation to escape agony. My favourite line was "Screw it! It can't get any worse." Then the change began. Which comes first, courage or commitment? It doesn't matter. They can happen simultaneously. I don't ever remember thinking, "Oh, I'm going to be courageous," in the moment. I just made the decision to make a change and did it. When I started, it would take extreme misery for me to make a change. For example, the pain of my friends shutting me out caused me to look at what wasn't working in my life and quit drinking. More recently, optimism and desire motivate me to change, like when I started my own business.

Coaching

Most of my major life shifts have had an important common denominator: I didn't do it alone. Timing is everything: when I was struggling to know my purpose, my husband introduced me to his coach, Aurora Winter. She was brilliant, determined, perky, and she had a program to help me find my "Million Dollar Message." I do well with programs, workshops and groups. Of course, knowing it was good for me didn't mean I wanted to do it.

Oh, how my resistance to something new awoke with the rage of a once-sleeping tiger. Streams of negative thoughts flooded my brain to keep me from moving forward. "I've done all this stuff before. My God! I could teach this course. It's a lot of money. It won't work for me..."

"Only what if it does work for me?"

What would my life be like if it did work for me? I would at last have the concrete block lifted from my chest and know what I wanted to do with my life. Imagine the dam, once holding back my power, bursting open to flood me with the energy for my purpose. What an incredible relief that would be. It would be worth any amount of money. It would even be worth doing what I was told.

I hated people telling me what to do.

I signed up with Aurora, and, as they say, the rest is history. She provided me with the structure to find my way to my own answers. She never gave me the solutions; instead, she held me while I did my own exploration. She had walked the path with many others to see their success and she guided me step-by-step along the way, knowing what could happen for me. She gave me the support I needed to have me stay until the miracle happened.

You would think that since I knew the way things work and what had been successful in the past, I would feel a rush of enthusiasm to dive in and get it done. Only that was not my experience, at least not in the beginning. I fought with myself and procrastinated about doing the work in her program. The fight with the old me, the old way of life, the old thinking was a turbulent inner battle. However, I wanted a new life and the pain of what wasn't working was excruciating enough that I was willing to do something different. I was straddling the space between what I was and what I wanted to be. That's the gift/curse of self-awareness: you witness yourself going through it. Does that make it easier? You tell me.

It was Aurora who had me take a look at my life with fresh eyes and contemplate my mother's assault from unexplored angles. After decades of trying, I had been close to transforming my reaction to that nightmare, only I had always fallen short. I needed a new way to investigate what happened. She challenged me to be willing to look for the good in the tragedies of my life. The concept wasn't new to me. One of my mantras is "Life is Learning," which I practiced with most things in my life. However, what I discovered was a hidden belief that some things were just too horrible to approach, things like assault, violence, death. I had a belief that it was impossible to change my thinking about those things.

With Aurora's help, the impossible became possible. I was able to look at the most significant horror of my life through the viewpoint of "Everything happens for my highest good." Not that what my mother went through was good, but that what I chose to gain from the experience was the training ground for my extraordinary life. Everything that happened in the subsequent years while I processed the pain, all that I learned, was fuel for my mission as a lightworker. I have the heart of a lion, with the vision to see through any darkness and guide clients to the light in their nightmare. I am not afraid of the dark anymore. Now the dark is afraid of me.

Me As A Coach

There are many reasons people ask for help besides not knowing what to do. Maybe you are scared to do it for yourself, you need an accountability partner to keep you focused, you need support pushing through the resistance, or you simply need someone on your side, not judging you, but championing you all the way. This is where a coach comes in.

I resisted the call to coach for about fifteen years. The first time I felt my desire to be a coach I was thirty-five, sitting in my three-storey walk-up one-bedroom contemplating my purpose. I remember immediately dismissing the idea. Why did I resist? I was terrified. I see now that I was paralyzed by the trepidation of wondering, "What if I do something wrong?" Helping people change their lives felt like a massive responsibility.

For many years I misunderstood what belonged to me and what belonged to the other. I consider myself an empath. It used to physically hurt me to watch other people suffer. I would do anything to help people feel better. I based my self-worth on my relationship to others, and I was always looking outside of myself for approval. My drive to help others used to be so strong that it was an unhealthy urge to save them. That was a painful place to be because I couldn't save anyone except myself. I wasn't ready to be a coach until I accepted that you are the only one who can change your life.

A coach is someone who sees all your talents, gifts and blindspots, whose only agenda is to love and guide you, tapping into a space of knowing that you too will one day awaken to the power and success within you. I call this space "The Knowing." It builds over your lifetime as those who love you contribute to the energetic stockpile. The truth of who you are is an invisible bonfire that explodes into life when you add your flame to the cache of matches that has waited for you to start the fire, and the explosion is unstoppable, burning brighter than you ever thought possible. Its warmth comforts you like the smile on your face standing in the spotlight of the sun. Think of the blanket of lighter flames at a concert; one ignites and then thousands are lit. Or the first candle that begins a vigil. One by one, candles light each other until the streets are aglow.

How I Coach

Every one of us has the answers to our own questions. Like a football coach or a sponsor from a Twelve-Step program, it's my job to lead you to your own answers. You need to find them for yourself and it's imperative you experience your own epiphany. When you have an aha, your brain releases dopamine, oxytocin and serotonin, providing a natural high. I think that's nature's way of rewarding you for doing all the excavation of your painful thoughts and feelings. You will always remember your revelation. We can easily forget advice from others, but when we find the path to the holy grail ourselves, we remember it. With a head full of happy chemicals, it's hard to forget what we discovered.

After all I've been through, I have the strength and confidence to support you to investigate the terrifying memories and overwhelming emotions that are blocking your success. After decades of searching, I've found an efficient way through intense emotions, and can guide you through the dark corners you've been avoiding to make sure you don't get lost there. I challenge you to take great risks for great rewards and I cheer for you all the way along. I dedicate my skills to your highest good and I invite you to look for your highest good in everything that happens.

This exploration provides you with a direct experience that opens a new way of thinking, along with visceral memories of how your insights unfolded. You will then have the delicious recipe for success baked into your body and mind, available to savour anytime.

Why did I choose coaching as my profession and not counselling or psychotherapy? I was called to be a coach because in my story it was coaching that transformed my life. For you, perhaps, it will also be coaching or perhaps counselling or psychotherapy or some other helping profession you are drawn to for support. Whatever course you choose, the essential piece is to get help.

It is impossible to solve the problem with the same mind that created the problem.

Albert Einstein

Recognizing the problem

Identifying Feelings

Sometimes the problem is crystal clear. It could be fear of the future or heartbreak after the death of a loved one. Other times it's a physical discomfort you can't quite name. After years of pushing down my emotions, I often struggled to identify what was bothering me.

In the early days, it could be excruciating pain in my chest, resulting from feelings I locked away for protection. I have learned to accept these body sensations as a doorway to unexpressed feelings. These days, I can easily identify universally accepted, basic human emotions like these: happiness, sorrow, disgust, anger, fear and surprise, which will lead me to more precise descriptions. The anger I feel may be frustration, aggression or hostility. The kind of fear I experience may be worry, insecurity or rejection. Other times, articulation of the experience eludes me and what comes out is sad, mad, glad or bad. Then my inquiry becomes about what kind of sad, mad, glad or bad.

Feeling Blocked

Another way to recognize problems is identifying the blocks in our lives. We may have a dream or a goal that we haven't realized yet. Finding out what's in the way of what we want exposes the problem from a different angle. When I wanted to enjoy my sex life more, I began working with Angela who helped me explore my past to find the obstacles to my pleasure.

When I was young, all I knew was that sex was dangerous, and I thought being beautiful was dangerous too. Back then, the story I told myself was women were in constant danger because men couldn't control themselves. That concept infuriated me. For my first sexual experience, I decided I would be the one in control. It made perfect sense to me that I should choose some stranger and just get it over with. I was incapable of accepting caring or romance in my world at that time. I refused to believe it was possible so whenever men were charming or romantic, I didn't take them seriously. I knew what they wanted, and they couldn't fool me.

That first sexual experience was completely calculated and alcohol-induced. I went to a bar, got drunk and picked up some random guy. We had sex and I didn't tell him it was my first time. I forgot his name and he insulted me with, "You could afford to drop a few pounds." That comment crushed me like a flower under a boot. Despite my calculated approach to the evening, losing my virginity was one of the most vulnerable moments of my life. I had no way to protect myself from his malicious words. I let his vision of me as a chubby girl taint my self-image for decades.

I found out later he was cheating on his girlfriend. They both worked at the local grocery store; running into them created enough drama for me to feel like a slut at the time. I was disgusted with him and simultaneously hungry for his affection and approval, even though I was pretending to be aloof. The whole thing felt ridiculous, pathetic and sad, leaving me furious with myself. Now I understand it was the best I could do with what I had. That's what I know today. Back then, I just hated myself, felt worthless and undeserving of anything better.

That experience left me vulnerable. Enter the older predator. He spotted me working behind the front desk of the hotel. He was at least twice my age, out of shape and not at all attractive. In any normal universe a beautiful young woman would have rejected his advances and sent him on his way. However, like any predator, he could smell the weakness in me, zeroing in on my low self-esteem and empathetic heart. That combination made me a prime candidate for his manipulation. He asked me out.

I agreed to meet him for coffee, and he proceeded to set his trap. He told me some heart-wrenching story about his wife dying after a long illness. He spun a compelling tale about his heroic care for her and his devastating loneliness now that she was gone. If only he could feel the touch of a woman again... I bought it lock, stock and barrel. Who would possibly lie about that sort of thing? Hearing his story, I felt his pain. Then he told me about his forlornness and how he just wanted to be touched. Would I ever consider spending time with him?

His plot was carefully orchestrated. It began with the idea of a Swedish massage and then it progressed to the suggestion of sex. He said he would pay me for my time; it was the least he could do. He gave me money for a cab to show me I could leave at any time. Only I didn't: I stayed, somehow hypnotized by an invisible force, probably my self-hatred.

How does this kind of abhorrent decision make sense to an otherwise intelligent young woman? I can tell you I remember being exhausted and extremely hungover that day. What I needed was sleep and a hot meal, time to recover from the previous night's escapades. What I got was a cunning old man with wicked intentions. Like any trapper, he was skilled at luring his prey into the perfect snare, and God knows he had my number.

I imagine he'd run this sort of scam plenty of times. An observer of human nature, he knew how to pick out his marks. I was physically vulnerable and spiritually unstable after a night of drinking and the recent loss of my virginity. I agreed to meet with him after work that day, thinking that having sex for money was a good plan. My heart goes out to that girl. There were a million signs for her not to do it.

The world was desperate to get my attention. The sky was black as night at 3 p.m. that afternoon as I left work, with hail pelting my shoulders as I ran through the brutal storm. I found out later that a tornado touched down in a trailer park just outside the city that day and killed fifteen people. Their trailers were flipped like the gods were using them as dice in a craps game. In total, twenty-seven people lost their lives in that storm. I could have seen that natural disaster as a sign, a way to get my attention, to wake me up and pry me from the clutches of that master manipulator. At the time, however, I was out of my body and numb to what was best for me. Nothing mattered. I didn't deserve anything good and I was determined to punish myself.

The world was an awful place full of awful people and here was the proof: a sinister grifter who had baffled my brains with his bullshit.

Although the signs were screaming for me to get the hell away from this pervert and get myself home, I accompanied him to a hotel room. He bought a bottle of Baby Duck for us. It was a cheap sparkling wine that my parents used to get for us kids on special occasions. It tasted foul. He was full of compliments about how beautiful I was. I can still see myself with my clothes in the bathroom: a yellow cotton skirt and a blue and white patterned, short-sleeved top that buttoned up in the back with a pretty ruffle that rested on the small of my back. I remember contemplating whether or not I needed to lose weight.

He was very experienced sexually but everything we did that day was new to me. Many things were pleasurable. Unfortunately, all of it was tainted because of the shame I felt since he had paid me to be there. When we were done, he took me home. Luckily for me, that's all he wanted and I never saw him again. Once I got home, I felt revolted that I had taken money for sex. I was physically, emotionally and spiritually bankrupt. I thought it couldn't get much worse.

I was wrong. It took a few hours for me to muster the strength to look in my purse for the money.

There was no money.

That's right. When I watched him go to my purse with money to pay me, he was pretending to put the money in my purse. Not only did he not pay me, he also took back the money he'd given me earlier for a cab home. The room was spinning. How could I have been so fucking stupid? I had let that loathsome bottom-feeder of a being take everything from me. I let him have my body and after the revelation of his masterful deception, I surrendered any confidence or self-respect I had left. I sat in the middle of my living room floor with another puke-green carpet in my fleabag apartment, completely humiliated. I hated myself with a renewed passion and dumpsters of shame poured over my soul. It would take until I was fifty and working with Angela to finally clear it all out of me.

I remember the suffocating shame I felt. What good could come from it?

What if the shame around what happened with that predator was my body's way of saying,

Stop it! Don't do that ever again!

Shame is how we feel when we make ourselves wrong for something we've done. What if shame is a natural consequence to warn us from things that are detrimental to our wellbeing? Like burning your hand on the stove, shame is a painful reality check meant to keep you from hurting yourself or others by repeating destructive behaviour. What if a higher purpose for shame is to deter you from doing anything that damages your self-esteem? In my case, agreeing to sell my body for sex was a shocking blow to my esteem. I remember hating myself back then. It was like part of me wanted to punish myself because I believed I was a horrible person and I deserved horrible things. What if the higher purpose of my shame was to protect me from hurting myself with something so detrimental? I am thankful that, without clearly understanding the message of shame, I never did anything like that again.

I have heard many stories from people feeling shame about things like abuse, sexual assault or incest. The act of blaming yourself is most certainly injurious to your wellbeing. What if the higher purpose of shame is not to make you bad but instead to shock you, to repel both the idea that you are bad and the behaviour of punishing yourself for what happened? Like when you take a sip of sour milk and your instinct is to spit it out. I see the healing and peace happen for people when they stop hurting themselves by blaming and shaming themselves. None of us can change the past; however, we all have the power to change the way we think about the past.

Feel the shame, learn the message it has for you and let it go or suffer. I held onto my shame for decades and it burned inside of me. It burnt through my spirit like leaving my hand on the stove. The longer you leave yourself in the fire, the greater the damage, until it kills you. Shame is like that, only it pushes you to kill yourself like it did with my friend.

We need to release our shame to be happy. When you go into your shame, you want a guide to go in with you so you don't get lost there. Shame is the lowest emotion on Dr. David Hawkins' scale of emotions that measures their vibration. I think of it as "in the toilet" because it feels like shit.

In his brilliant book *Power vs. Force*, Dr. David R Hawkins explains the levels of emotion. He uses kinesthetic testing to provide measurements for emotional vibration. His scale starts at the bottom with shame measuring 20. Moving upward we find fear is 100, anger is 150, courage is 200, acceptance is 350, love is 500, joy is 540, and peace is 600, leading to enlightenment at the top of the scale measuring 700 to 1000. When I learned about this scale from my coach Aurora, she pointed out that courage was the turning point on the scale. When we have the courage to reach for a higher vibration we can change how we feel.

I couldn't face the shame I felt around what I did that day alone. I needed a coach to help guide me in and out of it. Knowing you're not alone can give you the strength to do anything. Facing the shame from that experience took the power out of it. Like Dorothy in the famous scene at the end of The Wizard of Oz, I've looked behind the curtain to discover I am the one pulling the strings. All my emotions, no matter how intense or overwhelming they seem, are all simply parts of me with a message to help me. Today I help others go inside and face the parts of themselves that have been waiting for their attention to move them toward their highest good.

Turn your wounds into wisdom.

Oprah Winfrey

The Dark Side Of Unresolved Feelings

I believe that we all come into the world as light. Some souls leave as Mother Teresa, other souls leave as John Wayne Gacy. What's the difference? I believe it's a choice. Mother Teresa witnessed the extreme suffering of others compelling her to take action. The level of poverty and despair surrounding her could not have been comfortable; still she chose to be a messenger of Love and Hope, taking on impossible odds. Her choice was not the easy road, not the obvious one.

Looking from the incredible goodness of Mother Teresa to the incredible cruelty of a serial killer, I am curious about the possible impact of childhood abuse in twisting someone into such an aberration. There have been a number of books on the subject, and this online article https://bit.ly/abuseandserial is fascinating.

I am certainly not excusing the incomprehensible actions of these individuals. However, I can't help but ponder how a beautiful, innocent soul comes into this world and leaves it as a murderous butcher. These examples and the stories I've heard demonstrate the impact of unresolved harrowing childhood experiences. Their brutal internal suffering drives individuals to lash out at others or themselves. I used to ponder if my parents ever wondered the same thing about me. I looked like the same delightful girl they raised, only I was acting out like someone possessed. Thankfully, I am no serial killer, yet I have my own knowing of what it was like to be tormented by my childhood.

We all have choices on how we act or react based on the experiences we've had. We can see our growth in terms of the nature vs. nurture debate. My hatred of myself and the world was the nurture part of my evolution. The nature side was a light within me that was always there, powerful and fighting to stay alive in spite of the anguish of witnessing the depths of people's cruelty to one another.

Uncovering Your Victim

For any painful experiences of violence, abuse or neglect in my life, there was a victim identity. This was the part of me that felt powerless and hopeless after what happened. Even a deep disappointment could result in a feeling of being a victim. I remember feeling exhilaration over an upcoming trip with a beloved relative that plummeted into discouragement with their last-minute cancellation. I felt devastated and never wanted to feel that bad again. I decided, then and there, that looking forward to things or getting my hopes up was too painful. At a young age, I learned to bury these reactions of being shattered, embodying the victim like a secret twin.

The stories we make up about what happened to us create our thinking and behaviour. Change only begins once we start looking at our stories and uncovering the emotions behind them. For years, I told myself the story that it was my fault my mom was attacked. I was the only one who would blame my twelve-year-old girl for not stopping a thirty-something-year-old man from violating someone. That story was outrageous.

I needed outside help to uncover the victim inside waiting for my attention. With guidance, I began exploration to make the unconscious conscious. Parts of me were frozen after something bad happened, parts were maimed, blamed or shamed. After key experiences in my childhood, I made decisions to protect myself, decisions that became belief systems, beliefs like "The world is an unsafe place." "Adults or authority can't be trusted." or "Men are pigs who'll violate you if they think they can get away with it."

My natural defense mechanisms stopped working and became blocks to my happiness. My knee-jerk reactions were based on past experiences rather than what was happening in the moment. For example, I was unable to get excited about winning a trip to California through my work when I was thirty. I remember my boss's reaction when she gave me the news.

"My goodness, Heidi. This is cause for celebration. You look like your dog just died." At the time, I was frozen. Now, I recognize that when my reaction is disproportionate to my current circumstances, chances are I've triggered something from the past.

What Do You Want?

God grant me the serenity
To accept the things I cannot change;
Courage to change the things I can;
And wisdom to know the difference.
Living one day at a time;
Enjoying one moment at a time;
Accepting hardships as the pathway to peace;
Taking, as He did, this sinful world
As it is, not as I would have it;
Trusting that He will make all things right
If I surrender to His Will;
So that I may be reasonably happy in this life
And supremely happy with Him
Forever and ever in the next.
Amen.

Serenity Prayer – Full Version Reinhold Niebuhr

The key to achieving any goal is knowing the reason behind the goal. Knowing what you want will give you the energy you need to stay on your path when you are exhausted and ready to quit. When I was getting sober, what I wanted was some peace. I said the Serenity Prayer at meetings and many times throughout the day, only I didn't have any idea what serenity was. I knew the definition of the word, but the feeling of serenity was like a foreign language. My life was full of anxiety run by a tortured mind, and I was desperate to trade that in, longing for calm and stillness. It was that desperation that reached for me like a hand from the future, grabbing me and pulling me through The Twelve Steps I needed to change my life.

The serenity prayer was a quick, easy way to focus my thinking on what I wanted.

Before I even start coaching my clients, we talk about what they want. This is an exciting part for me because often people haven't given themselves time to dream and consider what they want. It's not just about quitting smoking or losing weight. It's about living a life in alignment with their true self or getting back to a version of themselves they can be proud of again. What they want needs to be something they want so badly they'll do anything it takes to have it. Knowing their deep desires empowers my clients to persist with our exploration when we uncover the monsters of their past. They are not alone. We do it together. I guide them through the darkness of overwhelming emotions, where they face their demons to discover a gentle ally inside. We celebrate their courage to stay the course, which will reveal insights necessary to fulfil their dreams.

In the beginning, my dream was serenity. Today my choice not to drink is about being the most vibrant iteration of me possible. Reaching for the higher goal of pure health, I find that anything out of alignment with my vitality is easier to resist and it simply falls away. It is only once I reach for something higher, beyond what I think I'm capable of, that I tap into the latent energies in myself and the Universe.

Recently, I began pushing myself beyond my limits in physical exercise. This was a major shift for me. In the past when I heard others raving about how exercise energized them, I didn't get the hype because that didn't happen for me. By reaching past my comfort zone, I am at last enjoying the "high" I heard so much about. The results are more subtle for me: a feeling of "not tired" rather than energized, more clarity of mind and increased stamina. The payoffs of a tighter butt and feeling more powerful are terrific; however, the secret bonus I didn't expect was the rush of healthy pride that comes from keeping my word to myself. Following through on my commitment to the new me boosts my self-esteem daily. My old story was that I didn't run unless someone was chasing me, I was allergic to exercise and had zero interest in a regular routine. My new story is that I am a vibrant being. It only makes sense that I would work out regularly.

I am happy to live an alcohol-free life and grateful to say that I don't have cravings for alcohol anymore. However, thoughts of drinking occasionally pass through my mind; how could they not? Everywhere in society there are messages about how great alcohol is. It's glamourized in the media and celebrated everywhere. When that happens, I simply remind myself how destructive alcohol was for my mental, emotional and spiritual health.

And just like that, the possibility of drinking again disappears. I choose not to drink. I've been making that choice one day at a time since 2004. Everytime I choose not to drink is an affirmation of how much I love myself and my life. It is always the best decision for my highest good. I have never once regretted the decision to not drink. How many things can you say that about in your life?

My experience with addiction has been black and white. Do it or don't do it. It's easy with life-threatening situations like drugs, alcohol and gambling. However, when it comes to things like sugar consumption, binge watching tv or using cannabis, I can tell myself it's not that simple. I watch myself as I dip into overdoing the behaviour and then stepping back into balance. None of these things are life or death. It's a finer point now. The question I ask myself regularly is, "How is this serving me?"

Take What You Like & Leave The Rest

In recent years I have experimented with CBD oil (Cannabidiol is a chemical in the Cannabis sativa plant, also known as cannabis or hemp), microdosing, psilocybin and cannabis edibles. The CBD oil was suggested to me as a natural alternative for pain relief after a car accident. I remember taking over-the-counter painkillers and being surprised at the impact on my body. After years of not drinking I was very in tune with my body and sensitive to any internal changes. I felt "spacey" and not like myself after taking the little blue pills so I was on the search for other options. I didn't experience much pain relief with the pure CBD oil and stopped taking it after a few times.

Microdosing is the practice of consuming very low, sub-hallucinogenic doses of psychedelic substances like psilocybin, found in certain mushrooms. I was drawn to explore this practice because of the proposed benefits for improved mental focus and support for creating new neural pathways.

My intention for experimenting with microdosing was to support the mental expansion I was experiencing, regularly moving into higher states of consciousness and acquiring insights with my work in Accelerated Evolution. I was curious about what positive effects the microdosing could have on this work; however, with my addictive history, careful consideration was required. A part of me was afraid of what might happen to me if I opened the door to taking mind-altering substances again. In the end, I determined for myself that the mushrooms did not present any danger of provoking my addictive tendencies. I remember enjoying greater focus while I was microdosing. I am always trying new health products to support my body and vitality. To me, microdosing felt very similar to any other vitamin or health supplement.

When I began taking cannabis edibles, I was exploring them as a pain remedy. That was the story I told myself. However, I quickly realized that taking edibles not only relaxed my body so that I was less attuned to the pain, being so relaxed was also a lot of fun. The allure of the easy good time that edibles offered captured my attention for a while because it was a treat. At first there didn't seem to be any negative consequences; however, I always kept my "inner monitor" on duty. I was regularly asking myself this key question: "Do I need these edibles to escape my life?" As long as the answer was no, I felt safe to continue. Then I was reminded of this beautiful concept:

The goal isn't to be sober. The goal is to love yourself so much that you don't need to drink.

Anonymous

It reaffirmed for me that I want to create the most enjoyable experience possible in this life. Negative consequences like a spacey feeling and severe intestinal cramping ended my experimentation. I feel like this was a part of me inspiring myself to look at my behaviour and I appreciated the challenge to continue living an extraordinary life without edibles.

One of the greatest gifts of an alcohol-free lifestyle for me was now being able to remember all the fun times I enjoyed. Back when I was a drunk and a drug addict, the only way I knew how to relax was taking something. There were many vague memories of glorious laughing fits; however, I could never remember the specifics of what had me laughing so hard, which made them empty moments. The brilliant thing is that I have been having fun without any chemicals for years and so I know that it is completely possible.

For me, there is a special satisfaction in relaxing naturally and connecting with the fun, light part of myself. What joy! My core values include freedom and joy. I am so grateful to be free of addiction with a new powerful connection to my innate happiness.

What do you want?

When you picked up this book, what were you hoping to change?

Commitment To Yourself

Making big changes takes 100% commitment. I had no idea what it was to commit body and soul to something until I quit drinking. I struggled with commitment most of my life. I used to believe that if I never committed to something completely, I would have a built-in cushion against the suffering of disappointment. However, those thoughts of holding back to protect myself only kept me from enjoying the satisfaction and fulfilment that come from being all in. I was far more comfortable with the confusion of sitting on the fence, determined to make the right choice, while missing out on the learning that comes with making any choice. It was a crazy game. I know now that whatever choice I make is the right choice. Even when I make a mistake, I choose to learn something from it and I move on to the next thing. Success or failure, each is an important step on my path. I learn as I grow and I grow as I learn.

My commitment not to drink has proven to me what's possible when I put my mind to it. Step Three of The Twelve Steps is where you make your commitment. "Made a decision to turn our will and our life over to the care of God as we understand him." I remember contemplating this intensely. Only it isn't the head that makes it happen, it's the heart. Your heart is your will. The commitment isn't happening until you surrender and are all in. When you let go and fall backward knowing the Universe will catch you, that's the magic moment.

I remember one of those precious, peaceful moments. I am amazed that I remember the exact moment it happened. I was bending over to pick something up on the landing of the stairs to my apartment and looking at the carpet when I decided to quit my job as a registered assistant.

Once upon a time, before I was married to my husband, I worked for him as his assistant. I had the biggest crush on him. He was tall, dark and handsome with a quick wit and the kindest heart. Crush is the perfect term because he didn't feel the same for me. Seeing him day in and day out at work, knowing he didn't feel the same, was excruciating. My spiritual counsellor at the time reminded me that as long as I was focusing on him, someone who didn't want me, I would never find anyone else who did want me.

The time had come to surrender the dream of getting together with my boss and with the support of my counsellor I decided to quit my job. I remember hearing inside myself, "If he doesn't want me, there will be someone else who does," and feeling a silent tranquillity from this knowing. That moment of surrender was a miracle. In 2022, he and I celebrated our sixth wedding anniversary and fifteen years as a couple.

As many times as I've surrendered over the last eighteen years, I still struggle to surrender on command. Mentally, I know I need to surrender; I've witnessed the power a hundred times. Just thinking about it doesn't work. I need to take action. I have to make the leap with my eyes closed and reach out for the invisible. I give in to the Divine.

Think of the analogy of sitting in a car with one foot on the gas and one foot on the brake. You're going nowhere. Making a commitment is deciding to take your foot off the brake and go for it, allowing the gas to propel you forward into your future. The beauty and freedom of that moment will fortify you with the wisdom to strengthen your faith the next time you are faced with a big decision.

The incredible power of commitment is that it focuses all your energy into action. All your problem-solving skills, labour and fantasies, all the energy previously spent on catastrophizing, worrying and analyzing which decision to make are now poured into the creative force of whatever you wish to achieve. All the daylight hours and sleepless nights previously spent questioning which way to turn are now applied to your core ambition.

Seeing the success of commitment over and over proves to me it's worth every minute I spend moving in the direction of my highest intention and ambition. I know the power, freedom and ease that are unleashed with commitment. It's simple. When you have the courage to admit to yourself and the outer world what you want, your reward for commitment is momentum and support.

...if you do follow your bliss you put yourself on a kind of track that has been there all the while, waiting for you, and the life that you ought to be living is the one you are living. When you can see that, you begin to meet people who are in your field of bliss, and they open doors to you. I say, follow your bliss and don't be afraid, and doors will open where you didn't know they were going to be.

Joseph Campbell

Seeing this in action means once you admit your passions to the world, you enlist all the wisdom, skills and connections around you. It is never necessary to have all the answers. Knowing this enables you to commit sooner the next time. Making the commitment is the key to unlocking all the invisible support you need to realize your vision.

I remember committing to start my own business. I had no clue of what to do. I had no business degree. I had no clients. I had no idea where to start. All I knew was that I wanted to work for myself. I was trustworthy and hard-working and had decades of experience in administration. In a million years I would never have guessed that the first step would happen at a fundraising event. It all began at a party where my husband introduced me to one of his business acquaintances and we began chatting. I told her I was starting a virtual assistant business. She asked me how she could help me.

"Well, I need help getting the word out about my business," I replied sheepishly. She invited me to her Business Networking International (BNI) group, which was the step that led to another step and to another and so on until I had a successful VA business.

One of my favourite sayings in recovery is, "Don't quit before the miracle happens." Commitment keeps your butt in the chair of a Twelve Step meeting until the peace of not drinking overcomes the pain you don't want to feel. I've experienced it and I've seen it happen for others over and over again. The commitment is what gets you through to the dawn. Commitment means you spend all your creative energy on how you can do this. Once you try it, you'll see it is easier and more powerful than all the time you once invested in saying, "I can't do this." That's done. And what a relief. The new focus is, "I am doing this." All your energy is focused on how. It's about spending time in the solution instead of spending time in the problem.

What we focus on expands.

Your mind will obsess on whatever you focus on; it's a problem-solving machine. Again it comes back to your choice of words. When you're thinking, "I can't do this," your mind is looking for evidence to support your belief. Conversely, when you're thinking, "How can I do this?" it will find you the answers. Your commitment gives you the patience to wait for the answers and call in the troops, if necessary. You use your faith to stick with it, and in the end your faith is rewarded.

Writing this book has taken me on a journey of commitment. The first step was having the guts to say out loud to the world, "I am writing a book." Since I said that, I have had many people help me along the way, and certainly the journey looks completely different than I imagined.

I thought it would be a matter of months and it became a matter of years. Still I kept going. I look back on all the hours I spent writing, the ink rolling onto endless pages, not knowing how it would all fit together. Still, I kept going, waiting for the miracle to happen, with no idea how it would. I never questioned my commitment; the decision was already made, so there was no going back. It didn't matter how long it took, or the detours along the way. I let go of the outcome and kept putting one foot in front of the other. Sure, I was frustrated during the process, but still I kept doing what needed to be done, one step at a time until my miracle happened: a published book and a reader to hold it.

Thank you for being part of my miracle.

Commitment To Expression

Throughout my life, writing and speaking have been powerful tools for healing and exploration. It is fascinating to me that so many of us resist using writing in this way. I often hear people say, "I am not a writer." I, myself, said that for years. However, you don't need to be a "writer" to use writing as a way to heal. Julia Cameron is the master for this message.

Her book *The Artist's Way* is a bible of instruction on using writing to access your creativity. She shares some beautiful spiritual principles about creativity. My personal experience with writing is that it takes me out of my mind and into the interior of myself instead. It is a practice. It is a journey into my own world of creativity. It is a way to tap into my inner wisdom and peace.

I've often heard experts like Cameron recommend handwriting over keyboard typing. There is science behind why handwriting is so powerful. Researchers have found that areas of the brain correlated with working memory and encoding new information are more active during handwriting. Individuals retain information better and activate more complex neural connections. Handwriting increases neural activity in certain sections of the brain, similar to meditation. We can access a different part of our being through writing. That is not about being a Pulitzer prize-winning author although that could happen. It is about using creativity to understand and express yourself more deeply.

Writing is an action. It is a crucial part of self-discovery. When you write, you are taking action to move forward. A cornerstone of recovery is doing The Twelve Steps. "Doing" is writing about each of the steps, answering questions to lead you down a path of contemplation into different areas of your life. I ventured into pondering people, places and things I would never have examined otherwise. The reward for all the triggers and discomfort was uncovering the self-destructive patterns that supported my addiction. For me, the writing was magic. There are other important physical actions in The Twelve Steps like making amends to those you have harmed, but even this step begins with writing.

The ink flows from your pen as your hand records the conversation you're having with yourself and the page, yourself and God, or yourself and your subconscious. The free writing that Cameron refers to as "The Morning Pages" is the practice of letting go of judgement or the need to edit what is flowing out of you onto the paper. Once you are able to relax your "inner editor," the truth comes out and your ideas flow freely. Some of them may be drivel, only I promise you that some of them are also brilliant.

My writing coach for this book, Junie Swadron, has a motto: "Your soul meets you on the page and something shifts. You begin to stand taller and one day you notice that your voice on the page becomes your voice in the world." She says this comes when you let go and let the writing do the writing.

For a long time, my working book title was *Write Your Own Adventure*. I loved the *Choose Your Own Adventure* books when I was growing up. Those books are all about making choices that change the outcome of the story. Each different choice brings you to different outcomes which lead to new endings, and that's the fun of it. I loved the power that it gave me. Those books were one place where I could see the impact I had on the situation. I can still feel the glee. Even though I changed the title of this book, I am suggesting that you "Write Your Own Adventure" as a way of life and of finding happiness in the wreckage of your past, like I did.

With writing, you have the power to access your inner guidance with paper and pen. Like any practice, the more you do it, the easier it becomes, keeping in mind that spiritual practice is about surrender. As I sit here with pen to paper, I notice I am experiencing surrender. Every one of us who practices anything—yoga, meditation, morning pages—knows there are good days and bad days. Days when we feel deep peace and connection and days when we are constantly distracted by the dog, a fly, or what to make for dinner.

If you surrender to an experience or emotion,
you stop trying to prevent or control it.

Cambridge Dictionary

Surrender is its own spiritual practice. The more I "try" or force it, the more it slips away from me. I hear Yoda's voice:

Try not.
DO
or do not.
There is no try.

Yoda

It is about letting go of control completely. Each time I surrender feels like the first time. Writing today, I am reminded that making a commitment to surrender is the simplest approach. Consider the analogy of skydiving: you commit to jumping out of the plane and surrender to gravity and the invisible air.

To surrender, I must completely let go of the outcome. I remember visiting my parents just before the Celebration of Love my husband and I had scheduled. After almost a decade-long tug-of-war over whether to be legally married or not, I had conceded to my husband's desire for no legal marriage. He agreed to an engagement ring, a party to celebrate with all of our friends, and a wedding dress. I told myself it was almost the same thing… However, as I prepared for the event, choosing a dress, finding shoes, deciding how to do my hair, all the fun things that were part of the plan, I noticed I wasn't as happy as I had expected to be.

When I went to visit my parents before the ceremony, I knew that they had assumed we would be legally married, and part of my trip would be explaining what we meant by "Celebration of Love" before they travelled to our event. I was nervous about telling them the truth and found myself struggling for the right words. My parents are old-fashioned and I knew that they wouldn't approve. The three of us were sitting at the kitchen table having a cup of coffee, still in our pyjamas. Everyone was calm and we were having a pleasant exchange while Mom and Dad were patiently waiting for me to get to the point. When I finally managed to say out loud, "It's not a legal ceremony," they didn't understand me at first.

My dad asked me, "What do you mean, it's not a legal ceremony?"

"I mean we won't be legally married."

With that, he leapt out of his chair and started pacing the kitchen.

"Jesus Christ! What the hell is wrong with him? You're telling me he's not marrying you? What the hell is the point of this? It doesn't make any sense."

And on and on it went. I can still see my dad, 5"8, medium build, olive skin, semi-balding with his hair trimmed very short to keep it tidy, wearing a white T-shirt and his blue plaid flannel pyjama pants. He was talking about respect, and partnerships and fifty-fifty, and how if Rob loved me he'd want that for me and I should dump him right now while I was still young and beautiful and I could find someone else who would treat me like I deserved.

Back and forth, back and forth, he was yelling and flailing his arms in the air, while my mom remained seated, doing her best to calm him down. Meanwhile, my head was swivelling left then right, following him like someone at a tennis match, as the tears streamed down my face.

Why was I crying?

It was like my dad was the voice of my own heart, speaking aloud all the thoughts and beliefs I had been afraid to admit to anyone, including myself. Needless to say, that conversation was a slap in the face, waking me up to my true heart's desire. When I left to go back home, I was not looking forward to the discussion I needed to have with Rob. Our celebration was to take place in just over a week. Everything had been planned. I had my dress, people were coming in from out of town, the caterers had been paid, the chairs rented. It was not going to be an easy conversation.

All I knew was that I had to surrender.

It was time to be brutally honest and have faith that it would be ok. I needed 100% commitment from Rob. For me, that meant a legal marriage, not a Celebration of Love, no matter how beautiful it would be.

Rob came to pick me up from the airport in great spirits and happy to see me. He was taking us home for a BBQ dinner. The meal was delicious, only it was difficult to enjoy since I had this big news to share. It was a bright August night with that perfect combination of not-too-hot, not-too-cold summer temperature, and so we ate outside. Rob noticed I was quiet and wasn't surprised when I said I wanted to talk to him.

I said something like this: "I want to tell you something. I feel like it will be a lot to process and I don't expect you to answer me right away. Please let me share what I have to say and then I'll leave you the space to consider it.

"After talking with my parents, trying to explain to them that a Celebration of Love is not a legal marriage, my dad flipped his lid. It made me think about what I'm doing and recognize how sad I am that we are not getting legally married. It's been bugging me for a while that I am not happier about all this. Going dress shopping, picking out shoes, finding the perfect caterer, I haven't been feeling the big excitement and delight that I was expecting for one of the happiest days of my life. You and I have gone back and forth over the years about being legally married. At one point, you agreed to the marriage and then it seemed to me that you were miserable every time we discussed the details of the wedding. It was no fun for me seeing you unhappy about the wedding and so, despite my desires, I proposed that we have a Celebration of Love which at the time felt like the perfect compromise.

"Except that it is my heart's desire to stand in front of our friends and family and declare my love and commitment to you and have it recognized by the whole world. I want a man who is proud to shout out to the whole world how much he loves me and wants to spend his life with me. I know that not wanting to marry me is not about how much you love me. We can love each other and want different things. I don't want to force you to do something you don't want. I have to be honest and say that I want more than a Celebration of Love. I accept that you don't want the same thing. I need to be true to myself.

"Now, I'll go to the other room and wait until you're ready to talk about this."

I was calm and I was kind. There was no anger or judgement in what I said. Then I went downstairs with my dog Harley, relieved to have all this out of my body at last and content with how I had expressed myself. I collapsed into my TV chair and Harley jumped up on my lap to cuddle.

Not long after, Rob came downstairs. I could tell he had been crying. He quietly reached for my left hand and slowly removed my engagement ring.

What have I done? I thought.

I was in shock and sick to my stomach. Then he bent down on one knee and began to deliberately place the ring back on my finger.

"Heidi Kuster, will you marry me for real this time?"

"Yes! Yes!" I fumbled to grab him and kiss him, awkward and clumsy with Harley in my lap. Then we all had a family hug.

Our wedding day was a true Celebration of Love. We held the ceremony and reception in our backyard with fifty of our closest friends and family. Tears of joy flowed that day as our guests witnessed the culmination of our nine-year courtship in our personal promises of love and devotion.

When I asked Rob about his experience of our wedding day, he said, "It was one of the happiest days of my life. If I had known how happy it would make you, I would have done it a lot sooner."

Hallelujah!

What We Focus On Expands

To write a book about my life, my struggles and what I've learned was a terrifying concept. Putting my ideas and experience on display felt like a major risk. "What if people don't like what I have to say?

What if my words trigger some people?" The more I thought about my fears, the worse I felt, and you guessed it—the less writing I did. Putting my attention on what I didn't want, knowing that what I focus on expands, I created more triggers for myself. When I expect "it," whatever "it" is, that's what happens. I find what I'm looking for. When I was looking for reasons not to write a book, that is exactly what I found.

I learned that a shift in perception is a miracle from Marianne Williamson's A Return to Love. Now I understand that the practice is to look for what I want rather than what I don't want. When I started my coaching practice, I remember having it backwards. It is easy to fall into that. I was focused on all the people who didn't want to work with me, people who didn't believe the same things I did, all the people who said "No" to my coaching. I was running around trying to convince them. I kept hearing from other coaches that I needed to be thinking about what I did want. That's when the light went on: change your focus to the kind of clients you do want.

The truth is simple, like the children's story of the little engine that could. When I focus on how I can't do something, like ride a bike, thinking it over and over, it becomes a belief. I tell myself I can't ride a bike and so I don't ride one. That was my story for decades. Then one day I decided to look for a fun way to exercise and biking was suggested to me. It made me think: Is it true that I can't ride a bike? No. I was afraid to ride a bike and I had been telling myself for years all the reasons that it was scary: A car could hit me. I can't see that well. Drivers get angry with cyclists...all those thoughts.

I made the choice to start thinking about what might happen if I said, "I can ride a bike." There is a bicycle trail right outside my house. I have friends who like to ride bikes. There are many bike trails in the city where I live so I won't be on the street with drivers."

I loved the idea. It excited me to think about the freedom I would have riding my bike and not waiting for a bus or a ride from my husband. I focused on the freedom and fun I wanted, then off I went to buy a bike. Miracle of miracles, one of my friends decided she wanted to buy an e-bike as well. When my husband tried my e-bike, it was so fun he decided to buy one, too. I enjoy summer in a whole new way riding with friends, getting in shape, enjoying all the sights and smells of my beautiful city. In recovery, all it takes is "a desire to stop drinking." In transformation, all it takes is a "desire to stop thinking the old way."

Resistance

No matter how good something is for you, there can be resistance. Sometimes the better it is for you, the stronger the resistance. It can be something like, "Oh, just one more episode of my favourite Netflix show. Oh, just one more potato chip. Oh, just one more phone call..." Sometimes resistance looks like using things that are good for you to keep you from reaching your goal. The voice that says the laundry needs doing, the kids need me, my friends need my help. I "should" be doing this or that. Anything that gets in the way of what you want to be doing, like writing your book, losing weight, training for a marathon, that's resistance. It puts anything you can think of in the way of getting what you want, such as guilt, shame, judgement, frustration or being overwhelmed.

Resistance springs from the survival part of you constantly looking for anything that threatens your safety. What's safe? Things you know, things you have done over and over without harm. When you have something you want that's new and unknown, there is a part of you that does not want to do things differently because the ancient premise that kept you alive was "the unknown is life-threatening." Even if the unknown is good for you, like being sober, losing weight, or expressing your creativity, your survival instinct is to resist the danger of the unknown. This is The Reptilian Brain we're talking about. T. Harv Eker likens it to your bodyguard.

A bodyguard has a job to do and has no time for your bullshit. You can't reason with them or charm them. They are completely single-minded. Everything is about protection and safety. They see everything as a threat. When the bodyguard walks in the room, he's not looking for friends or checking out the food; he's checking the exits and scanning the crowd for potential threats.

It's nothing personal. That's his job. It's the same with your lizard brain. It is the hardwired part of you whose job it is to keep you alive.

The Reptilian Brain is commonly described as the part of the brain looking after our major survival instincts: the four Fs; feeding, fight, flight and, well...let's just call it reproduction. It is made up of the basal ganglia (striatum) and brainstem at the back base of your skull. It is the oldest part of your brain, the part that has lasted from the earliest stages of human's physical metamorphosis, back to the time when we were walking on all fours. Our physical transformation is a long way from those days and yet this ancient part of us lives on in its fundamental focus to keep us alive.

This part of us is hardwired with a life-or-death perspective. Like martial law in times of war, it has the supreme power to shut down the creative, problem-solving frontal cortex and take over your physical body to protect you. If you've been triggered and unable to perform as you wish, you should be asking questions: Why am I shutting down? Why can't I move forward? What am I afraid of? How can my body betray me? Why am I not listening to myself? Why can't I make myself do what I want?

Using Emotions To Your Advantage

There are three steps to dealing with resistance, also known as emotional blocks, or whatever is getting in the way of what you want. They are:

Awareness Acceptance Action

Everything begins with awareness. Recognize there is resistance. It's natural. Give yourself a break about it. Now that you understand resistance is your friend rather than your enemy, you can work together to get what you want. The way to work with this valuable defense system is to remove the threat. All of our powerful relationships work best with clear communication. When your base self understands there is no threat, it will cancel martial law and return the power to your frontal cortex, allowing you to do as you wish, to take action and move forward in the direction you choose. How do you convince yourself there is no threat? You open a dialogue with yourself and allow those powerful emotions to have their say. Put your attention on your resistance. What are your feelings trying to tell you?

Let me use my relationship as an example. When I am trying to "make" my husband do it my way, he digs his heels in and fights harder to defend his position. When I accept him and his position, it is natural to treat him as an ally rather than an enemy and practice my intention to understand his position without trying to change it. In those moments, I notice he also relaxes and opens to understand my position better. Our dialogue goes from a fight to an open and loving conversation.

At the start of Covid I went to my husband to discuss a big purchase. I was calm and clear on my position so I went to him to communicate the details and listen to his point of view without any attachment to the outcome. I was relaxed and offered a concise explanation as to why the purchase was a good idea. When he shared his reasons for why the purchase was not a good idea, I listened to him with love in my heart, accepting him without judgement. I didn't try to change his mind, I accepted his no to making the purchase.

His reaction was to relax his guard and take more time to contemplate my point of view in order to better understand my position. In the end, he accepted my idea as something that was actually in alignment with what he wanted. We mutually agreed to make the purchase and we have both been delighted with the outcome and how it has served us.

Exploring Fear

I had a brilliant experience working with another coach, exploring my fear about publishing my book. My practice these days is to go directly into my emotion and feel it as strongly as I can. Some would call this counterintuitive. For me, it is the exact opposite of how I grew up dealing with my emotions. There was a time when I was tormented by the intensity of my emotions. I would do anything to escape the pain and suffering that overcame my being, body and soul. In contrast, this experience was an easy journey led by a loving guide to connect me with a piece of myself that happened to be afraid.

At first I felt it in my body, a tension and rigidity in my chest and solar plexus. I relaxed into an internal exchange with my fear. My intention was to feel the fear as strongly as I could while my coach was asking me questions. In the beginning, the images were of me as a frightened child. I was running around desperately searching and feeling confused. I didn't know who I was. I kept feeling it as strongly as I could, and moment by moment the fear was dissipating. I was watching the darkness of the fear getting smaller and smaller while I noticed the light and peace more and more. It was like the light and peace were still and the fear and darkness dissolved into the peace. It felt natural and happened effortlessly.

During that exercise I was on a journey with my fear. We were together, each of us having a unique experience. I had no desire to run from the fear or to make it go away. I had no need to cut it off or judge myself for it or even make it evil or wrong. I listened to my fear and I am grateful for the secrets it shared with me, granting a novel perspective. The fear was gone. I felt calm, at peace and confident: I was ready to move forward.

I am grateful to be able to accept and embrace my emotions. I love myself and all these endless pieces of me that I uncover over time. Every new introduction is an opportunity to accept myself more and a chance to deepen my peace and expansion. This is my spiritual path.

Better is possible.

PART TWO
Triumph

Flip The Script - Give Up Being The Victim

I want to dive deeper into the details of the exercise that transformed my point of view on tragedy. I was working in a mastermind group with coach Aurora Winter who asked us to write out six turning points in our lives. Just the facts, no detail or embellishment. The bullet points came easily to me and it began as a seductively simple exercise.

These are the original passages I wrote:

1. Mom's assault. I was 12
2. Moving to BC. I was 25
3. Getting sober at age 35
4. Meeting Rob at age 29, working for him age 37. Marrying him age 47
5. Starting my VA business age 42
6. Mom's illness age 47

The next part of the exercise was to tell the story of the six bullet points from a victim's perspective. It would be a kind of "woe is me, I had it so hard" story. The last step was to give your story a catchy title that summarized it. Here's what I came up with...

Victim story - "Angry and Addicted"

I witnessed my mother's assault when I was 12. This shattered my spirit for many years. I was an angry person for many years. At age 25 I was living in Edmonton and my life was going nowhere. I had a dead-end job and a dead-end boyfriend. I took a marketing and management course but couldn't get a job so I moved to BC. Life in BC was full of partying and drugs. My best friend cast me out because of my alcoholic behaviour. I went to a personal development seminar thinking I had mental health issues. It turns out I was just an alcoholic. So I got sober.

Met Rob Smith when I was 29. I was convinced he was out of my league. At 37 I started working for him and eventually fell in love with him. He wasn't interested in a relationship which broke my heart. At 38 when I threatened to quit he started dating me. It was 9 years of personal growth and turmoil in our relationship until we married when I was 47.

At age 42 I started my own virtual assistant business and proceeded to go into massive debt when my income couldn't keep up with my spending.

At 47 I signed a consumer proposal claiming bankruptcy.

After a long battle with cancer my mom died.

Then came the eye-opening experience of using the same facts to tell the story from a hero's point of view...

Hero's story -

I witnessed my Mother's assault when I was 12. This heart-breaking incident deepened my empathy and emotional intelligence. I was able to heal my anger and open my heart to the love of an incredible, kind, sensitive man.

Men and women were drawn to confide in me their stories of abuse. Because of what I had been through I was strong enough to witness their experience. I could bear the pain and hold them in love. I was able to remind them this was not their fault. All this exposure to pain and tragedy deepened my already existing empathy and expanded my emotional intelligence. I sought out all the healing I needed to move from being shut down and furious with men; a woman who believed that all men were pigs and would assault you if they could get away with it, to an open-hearted woman, who believes there are kind and loving men in the world and is ready for love.

I lived with my family for six months, holding all of us in love throughout Mom's illness.

After all the work I had done, I was surprised to see Mom's assault at the top of my list. I remember it coming up and having thoughts like, "Are you kidding? After everything you've done? Why would you bother putting it on the list?" Even so, I let go of all the questions and decided to trust my intuition, writing the first thing that came to me. I put my attention on what happened with the conscious intention to see things differently. If I could change the way I thought about that night, I could change the way I thought about anything.

See Resources at the back of the book for Six Bullet Exercise.

How Do You Want To Feel?

Raising Your Vibration

We can use our physical body to change the way we feel. Sometimes after meditation I stand up in a power pose with my arms raised to the sky, saying my massively transformative purpose (another precious lesson from my coach, Aurora).

"I am raising Humanity's vibration by being myself and speaking my truth.

"I am spreading transformation and joy through humour and lightness."

This is what I want and how I want to feel. My thoughts become feelings and my thinking shapes my mood, which dictates my behaviour. A practice of setting my intention gives me thoughts to focus on to shape my day and experience.

Raising your vibration is a natural inclination. Think about it... It is common knowledge that when people are feeling bad they are "feeling down" and experiencing lower emotions like shame, guilt, grief, fear or anger. What do you want to do for them? You want to "Cheer them up." There is the intuitive knowing that feeling good is going up and feeling bad is going down. Hawkins gave me a visual of this with his Ladder of Consciousness.

I have known for years that dancing makes me feel better. All personal development workshops I've attended used movement and music to raise the energy. These days I often hear about coaches making movement a part of their coaching philosophy.

When people are "up" they are open, playful, willing to engage with you; when people are down, maybe tired or bored, they are less willing to engage. Try it some time. I invite you to practice using music and dance to energize yourself. Movement gets your juices flowing. You are moving and going into your body where you can feel your breath and blood moving through you. That is your life energy. Connecting with movement and music, you can't help but cheer yourself up. All you fans of the TV show "Grey's Anatomy" know about "dancing it out" to shake off a bad day. Movement and even posture can also alter how I feel.

Power Pose

 What do I mean by "power pose"? Social psychologist Amy Cuddy's TED talk is an informative presentation about non-verbal communication. What got my attention was her explanation of how changing our posture can change our thoughts and feelings.

She studied power and dominance across the animal kingdom and discovered it is all about expanding and opening up. Imagine a runner crossing the finish line. They have their arms in the air like a V, with their chin up. This is a universal expression of triumph, the power posture of victory, whether people are sighted or blind. When we feel powerful, we spread out and take up a lot of space. When we feel powerless, we do the opposite. We try to make ourselves smaller by doing things like slouching and making tiny movements.

I look back to when I was feeling insecure about my body and unsafe drawing attention to myself: I was slouching and rolling my shoulders forward to hide my breasts. I felt self-conscious whenever I tried standing tall, shoulders back, walking with my chest out. Over the years, with meditation and my personal development work, my posture has improved immensely. I spend more time feeling confident, walking with a straight spine and my head held high.

Cuddy's work explains that we can influence how powerful we feel with our movement. When I heard Cuddy's presentation on using your body to feel powerful even when your mind doesn't, it gave a whole new meaning to the saying, "Fake it til you make it."

She did an experiment with two groups of people. The first group spent two minutes daily in a power pose (my favourite is called

"Wonder Woman" where you stand, legs hip-width apart, hands on your hips, straight back and shoulders, chest out) while the second group spent two minutes in a lower power pose (folding up, making yourself small like sitting with your shoulders rolled forward and your arms crossed). They measured the participants' levels of testosterone (power hormone) and cortisol (stress hormone) before and after the posing. The results from the experiment revealed that after two minutes in a power pose participants' testosterone levels were higher and the cortisol levels were lower. People spending two minutes in a low power pose saw a drop in their testosterone levels and a spike in their cortisol levels.

Your hormones impact how you feel: with higher testosterone and lower cortisol you will feel more assertive, confident and comfortable, whereas with lower testosterone and higher cortisol levels you will feel more stressed, reactive and shut down. All this can happen in only two minutes a day. Cuddy proves with her experiments that our bodies have the power to change our minds and our minds change our behaviour.

The Power Of Choice

Jane came to me because her anxiety felt out of control. She was losing sleep, feeling tense, even nauseous; she found herself overreacting with her fiancé, feeling jealous and acting suspicious. She had gone from a carefree, fun partner to an uptight, cranky, jealous partner: as you can imagine, it was negatively affecting her relationship. In our work, it quickly came to light that a core issue needing her attention was a betrayal from a past relationship.

In the previous situation her intuition was telling her that something was going on; however, her partner kept assuring her that wasn't the case. Instead of trusting her intuition, she was questioning herself, feeling stupid and denying her inner wisdom. Later, she discovered he was, in fact, cheating on her; she wasn't crazy and her intuition had been right all along. Now, in her new relationship, she had all these suspicions of infidelity tormenting her, even though logically she was sure her current partner was faithful.

Jane was suffering emotionally, mentally and physically from these conflicting stories in her mind. She told me she was watching herself overreact when her partner went out for drinks after work. She was interrogating him and checking his phone behind his back; she said it was like "she couldn't help herself."

She was willing to try anything, even reliving the past. Jane had locked away feelings of betrayal. Those unexpressed emotions from a previous partner's infidelity kept pulling her out of the present healthy relationship, into the past where she reacted with jealousy and irrational behaviour. Through our work, she was able to express and explore those feelings and dissolve their hold over her. Coming from this new place of peace, it was easy for Jane to choose new thoughts and beliefs to nourish her current relationship. In a matter of weeks she was back to the carefree, confident woman she wanted to be, happier than ever in her relationship.

We can change our brains, resulting in a change in our behaviour. The brain's ability to adapt is called neuroplasticity.

> Neuroplasticity refers to the physiological changes in the brain that happen as the result of our interactions with our environment. From the time the brain begins to develop in utero until the day we die, the connections among the cells in our brains reorganize in response to our changing needs. This dynamic process allows us to learn from and adapt to different experiences.
> Dr. Celeste Campbell

What does that look like? Our brain creates neural pathways for our behaviours and beliefs. A neural pathway is a series of connected neurons that send signals from one part of the brain to another, like a passage in the nervous system. I see my brain covered in neural pathways like the earth covered in highways. Travelling down the same road over and over entrenches a neural pathway so that it becomes automatic and takes little energy to execute. For example, if you are someone that drives the exact same way to and from work, it can happen that you arrive home and don't remember how you got there. You were on "automatic pilot."

To change our behaviour requires focused effort to shift direction and go down a different road. It takes a lot of energy to do things differently. When I travel the new road enough times, it becomes the regular route. The brain is all about using the body's energy efficiently; therefore, when it registers that a neural pathway is no longer being used, the brain will fill it in rather than wasting the energy of maintaining the unused path. Not only is it possible to change your behaviour, the new behaviour is sustainable.

For Jane, choosing a different route meant choosing to focus on different thoughts. When she had the urge to check her fiancé's phone, she noticed the thought, accepted it and chose to focus on contrary thoughts. Jane would remind herself that she trusted her partner, that her partner loved her and they were happy together. This new way of thinking empowered her to follow through with acting like the trusting partner she wanted to be. Once she had cleared the suspicion and jealousy left over from her previous relationship, she was free to focus on her current loving, trusting relationship. The necessary actions to nurture her relationship became clear and easy.

Our lives are made up of the stories we tell ourselves over and over. Once the jealousy was gone, Jane could choose a new story: "I am a trusting and loving partner." Claiming that new story, saying it over and over, focused her attention on the actions of a trusting and loving partner. Today Jane is happily married.

There was a time when my preferred escape from anxiety was the numbness of crack cocaine. Critical thoughts constantly spun through my mind like a pointed mediaeval ball and chain, leaving me a bloody mess. The drugs were a welcome reprieve from my torment. All I cared about was the time when I could be free of the anxiety, self-hatred and worry. I began lying and stealing to support my habit, almost completely unconscious of what I was doing and what I was becoming.

Honesty and integrity are core values for me; my crack addiction ended when I realized I was no longer behaving like an honest person. I remember sitting in the pink walls of our breakroom at work, staring at the green pages as I struggled to balance the accounting ledger for our social committee. I was the social convener and the treasurer for our group. At that time, I was regularly "borrowing" money from the social fund to buy drugs before I deposited it to the bank. I was taking more and more money and it was getting harder and harder to pay it back. As I sat in the breakroom, for an instant the haze of my addiction lifted and I saw clearly the liar I had become. What if I couldn't get back to the honest person I once was? That moment scared the living hell out of me. My husband calls it a cold rush of shit to the heart. Whatever you call it, that was my sobering moment, the moment I chose to shift my focus from escaping my life and getting high at any cost, to getting back to myself before I lost every shred of who I was.

I needed to stop stealing immediately, which meant no more drugs. It was obvious to me I would need to change everything. The house where I lived was a party house so I moved away and disassociated with all my drug-taking friends, choosing instead to spend time with friends who didn't do drugs. Being in a brand new environment with new people, I was consciously creating a new routine without drugs. It worked and my crack addiction was terminated.

Changing our habits and our behaviour takes time, awareness, commitment and support. Once you've realized what you want to change and addressed the emotional blocks, it's a matter of committing to your new behaviour and choosing it over and over until it becomes your new normal.

I love this simple, illuminating story Wayne Dyer shared. It's called *Autobiography in Five Short Chapters* by Portia Nelson—singer, songwriter, actress and author.

Chapter I
I walk down the street. There is a deep hole in the sidewalk.
I fall in. I am lost... I am hopeless. It isn't my fault.
It takes forever to find a way out.
Chapter II
I walk down the same street. There is a deep hole in the sidewalk.
I pretend I don't see it. I fall in again.
I can't believe I am in this same place. But it isn't my fault.
It still takes a long time to get out.
Chapter III
I walk down the same street. There is a deep hole in the sidewalk.
I see it there. I still fall in...it's a habit...but, my eyes are open.
I know where I am. It is my fault. I get out immediately.
Chapter IV
I walk down the same street. There is a deep hole in the sidewalk.
I walk around it.
Chapter V
I walk down another street.

The Power Of Being Heard

In the early years of our relationship, I had a great deal of difficulty opening up to my husband. I didn't know how to let him into my life. I didn't know how to trust. I didn't believe he loved me. How could that possibly be true? What was happening in our relationship didn't match any of my previous experiences. I was programmed to react to men as if they were going to hurt me. It wasn't logical, it was all happening at a feeling level and it was exasperating for me as well as my husband.

A belief is simply a thought you think over and over. For decades I had been telling myself I was unlovable. It was another one of those beliefs running in the background just below the level of consciousness. I only started to remember it was there because I had a reason to question it...a reason to begin looking at my beliefs and my behaviours. My husband used to say, "How is it possible that you are scared to open up and trust me? I've never done anything but love and accept you."

That was totally true. My reply to him was that I had a lifetime of experience before him that I had to deal with. I have a lot of love and respect for that woman as I write this. However, I remember the moment when the conversation took place. It was on the telephone. I was living in my one-bedroom condo, lying on my white leather couch, staring at the vibrant red wall in my living room. I was physically unable to speak to him. Thinking about it now, I know my fear of what he would think or say triggered all the unexpressed fear from my past, which is why it felt so much bigger than my current circumstances. I was hitting the brick wall between reason and my feelings. I remember opening my mouth, only nothing came out. It wasn't logical. I was trapped in the silence of all my old experiences shutting me down. They stole my voice.

That wasn't the first time. I remember many instances like this; people wanted to help me and they were waiting to hear what I had to say while I sat there on the phone with my mouth open and nothing coming out. It's like that dream where you're talking, then screaming, and no one can hear you because no matter how hard you try, no sound is coming out of your mouth. I know now it was all self-imposed. Back then I had no idea of how to escape my silent prison.

"What in God's name was wrong with me?" The self-judgement was debilitating.

It was AA that began to thaw me out of that iceberg of silence. In The Twelve Step meetings you have the opportunity to speak without interruption. Each person can share what's going on, without fear of someone attacking them or arguing or telling them to shut up. For up to five minutes, you can open your heart and let anything recovery-related spill out of your mouth. People will sit and listen. No one is there to fix you. No one claims to have the answers. No one judges you, your feelings or experiences. They just listen. The healing that comes from being heard is magic.

In the beginning, I would go to meetings and just talk and cry. I was lost and needed direction, so when I was told to go to meetings

I clung to that. I listened to other people's experience, strength and hope, and I learned new ideas to try in my own life. They told me all the instructions I needed were in *The Big Book of AA*. I discovered it was full of examples of people who recovered, people who lived happy, productive lives without being drunk all the time. I could relate to most of their stories, which comforted me and perplexed me at the same time. Previously I had thought I was the only one suffering this way. I was grateful that so many people at the meetings shared truthfully and vulnerably about what it used to be like, what had happened, and what it was like now. I always left the meetings feeling inspired.

From a very young age, I have been curious about God. After my mother was attacked, my curiosity became a desperate quest to feel better, to make sense of it all. However, while I was drinking, drugging and self-destructing, none of the spiritual teachings I found seemed to work for me. I smile now when I realize that becoming an alcoholic and working through recovery are an important piece of the foundation of all my spiritual teachings. It makes no difference where you heard it first: Leonardo Da Vinci, the authors of Hay House, or Twelve Step recovery. All that matters is you hear it and let it in…

I have been impressed with the urgency of doing. Knowing is not enough; we must apply.
Being willing is not enough; we must do.

Leonardo Da Vinci

Indigenous peoples have an ancient communication tool known as the Talking Stick, used to facilitate listening for the sole purpose of understanding. The Elder in the gathering is the first to hold the Talking Stick. The one holding the talking stick is the only one allowed to speak. Everyone else listens in silence. The stick is handed around the group and everyone has a chance to speak until it is returned to the Elder.

My first experience with a Talking Stick was when I lived on a

First Nations Reserve in Canada. I had the good fortune to be invited to a house blessing ceremony because I was part of the community. I was a little uncomfortable about going since I didn't know the couple. My friend assured me that everyone was welcome. I am enamoured with ceremonies of celebration and I decided to go, despite my anxiety. At the beginning of the ceremony, there were blankets laid down as a pathway from outside to inside the house. Linda, the lady of the house, was the only one to walk the path and her footprints marked the "freshly fallen snow" of the blankets as she entered her new home. Part of the ritual was smudging the house, burning sage to clear any negative energy. The main part of the ceremony consisted of Linda standing in the centre of the circle, now covered in the blankets from outside, while the Talking Stick was handed to each person. Each individual shared their good wishes for the couple and their new life together. The room was filled solely with the speaker's voice and the love from all of us listening.

At the end of the ceremony, there were gifts for the group. Linda gave the blankets to people in the crowd. I was overcome with emotion when she chose to give me one. By the end, I was crying with joy. I have the blanket to this day. I call it my love blanket and I sit on it almost every day while I have my breakfast, enjoying the soft, morning silence.

As a coach, the cornerstone of my practice is the ability to listen without judgement and offer people love. Being seen and heard speaks to our need to belong and our need for safety. When others listen to us, we are included, connected, and we have an opportunity to have our needs met. I hold the space because giving another being a spotlight of love and understanding to speak their truth is magic. Holding them with care while they find their way to their truth is miraculous. In that space and time of love, people have lightning bolts of insight. They hear themselves and dive into truth they didn't know they knew. The Divine reveals whatever they need in that moment.

Your Best Is Good Enough

A powerful challenge in my life has been the struggle with "I'm not good enough." Don Miguel Ruiz's *The Four Agreements* is a brilliant book with simple truths that can change your life when you practice them. The author invites you to make four agreements with yourself:

> *Be impeccable with your word.*
> *Don't take anything personally.*
> *Don't make assumptions.*
> *Always do your best.*

The agreement to "Always do your best" was a game-changer for me. I used to beat myself up with my obsession for perfection. Nothing I did was ever good enough; I didn't believe anyone when they said something positive about what I'd done. It didn't matter whether it was kudos for a client project or what I'd made for dinner: in my mind, I was finding fault with my work. At the time, I couldn't even say positive things to myself. Part of Ruiz's Agreement was to accept that my best would change from day to day: some days my best is ten out of ten while others it is three out of ten. As long as I give 100% of my three out of ten, I am doing my best. Giving myself permission to allow my best to be fluid encouraged me to believe my best is good enough. That let me breathe again.

When I practice yoga and meditation, I embody the belief that my best is good enough. It is irrelevant whether I have a good meditation or bad meditation: all that matters is that I meditate. The rest will take care of itself. When I practice yoga, I appreciate the physical experience of being in my body. It is no longer about achievement, comparison or striving to be more flexible. For me, yoga is about enjoying the sensations that are happening in my body in the present moment. Once upon a time, I ran from a yoga class because going into the silence of my body and listening to the criticism inside was too painful; now I am comfortable in the silence and in tune with my body. I embrace the sheer pleasure of Shavasana: the end of your yoga practice where you reap the benefits of your labour and surender into complete relaxation.

Working as a solopreneur expanded my embodiment of my best being good enough. In the beginning of my virtual assistant business, there were times I actually destroyed projects trying to make them perfect: then I scrambled in desperation to recover what I had lost. I had an amazing aha when I heard the concept, "Done is better than perfect." This was a welcome addition to, "Always do your best," deepening my training and allowing me to be more productive rather than obsessive.

PHALT

My journey has been about getting comfortable in my own skin. Going into my body used to be an unpleasant experience because I was pushing down negative feelings as a way to cope. Alcohol and drugs were an easy escape from that discomfort. Setting aside those coping mechanisms, I was starting life over: a toddler in a thirty-five-year-old body, feeling raw and learning how to deal with life.

I am responsible for myself, my behaviour and actions. When I notice an emotional response to someone or something, the first thing I do is look at my part in the situation. One of my favourite recovery tools is HALT: it stands for hungry, angry, lonely, tired. As an addict I learned to use this self-survey when I was feeling weak and thinking of drinking.

In the beginning, I trained myself to ask, "Am I hungry? Do I need to eat? Am I tired? Do I need to rest? Am I angry or upset? Do I need to vent? Am I lonely? Do I need to connect with someone?" Literally, I would be counting on my fingers: H-A-L-T. I was learning about self-care and these questions helped me determine, "What's going on with me? What's happening here that I want to drink?" That craving for alcohol was the old behaviour of being desperate to escape how I was feeling.

Once I took the time to become self-aware and care for myself, I recognized my sensitivity to the inextricable connection between my physical sensations and my emotional experiences. When I ate something, took a break, did some journalling or talked to a friend, I felt better and the intensity of the craving disappeared. Today, when I notice my emotional reaction is disproportionate to the situation, I know it's an alert that I need some self-care. I may not be in danger of drinking but I am in danger of emotionally acting out.

After sustaining injuries in that car accident, I experienced chronic pain which exhausted me physically, mentally and emotionally. I had a lot less patience with everyone, especially myself. I remember being frightened by the cruel thoughts I had about my husband over the smallest thing. My nerves were raw and the slightest altercation could escalate into rage. I realized I needed to add "pain" to my checklist and I created a new acronym for self-care: PHALT.

I began asking myself, "What's at PHALT?" Am I…in pain, or hungry, or angry, or lonely, or tired? Any of these conditions could push me over the edge. When I feel vulnerable, my power to choose becomes precarious. In the case of being a recovering addict, the power to choose sobriety was threatened. In relationships, it was the power to choose kindness that was threatened.

This simple check-in, "What's at PHALT?" gives me a moment to pause, to breathe and then choose my actions rather than lashing out. Maybe, it's time for a snack, a nap, a break, an Accelerated Evolution practice or playing with my dog. The pause saves me from creating drama and hurting myself and/or others. This second of clarity can mean all the difference in the world. Is there a reason to be upset or am I blowing things out of proportion because I'm hungry? That's all I need to ask.

I often use PHALT as a relationship tool. My looking after myself has been known to save my husband from mortal danger. For example, when I find dishes on the counter instead of in the dishwasher… (I feel you nodding your head…That's totally annoying, right?) A good night's sleep or a snack can be the difference between putting the dishes away, reminding myself of all the great things my husband does for me (like cooking dinner, washing the dishes or rubbing my feet) or snapping at him, feeling like he is the most inconsiderate human being on the face of the earth, and wanting a divorce.

Using PHALT is a quick way to identify what I need to get back in balance where I feel calm and clear.

See Resources at the back of the book for PHALT Exercise.

What Anger Is Trying To Tell You

When I think about anger, I think about Marshall Rosenberg and his brilliant philosophy of Nonviolent Communication. At the core of his philosophy is the practice of listening without judgement, with the goal of understanding. Rosenberg talks about listening with the heart of a giraffe, which has the biggest heart of all land animals. I once bought a stuffed giraffe to remind me to listen with love. When I look at my 6'5" husband (the tallest human land animal I know), I am reminded of his huge heart and how he inspires me to listen more and talk less.

Another piece of Nonviolent Communication that I use constantly is the premise that all anger can be distilled down to an unmet need. Once that need is satisfied, the anger dissipates. Whenever I am vulnerable because I'm angry, I ask myself, What do I need? What am I missing here? I have no control over anything other than myself. Taking time to consider my needs shifts my focus from blaming the other person or situation to considering myself and what I can change. Maybe I'm angry because I need some help. I don't have to do everything by myself. Learning to ask for help rather than lashing out because I am feeling overwhelmed is a big life-saver for me. When I find myself resenting my work, it's usually because I feel overwhelmed. It's time to re-evaluate: "Does this need to be done right now?" Looking at my anger for information about what I need nurtures relationships with myself and others.

I've learned that conflict can be used to build intimacy. Conflict happens in relationships when needs are not being met. It is an opportunity to make a change, to pivot when things are not working.

When you are willing to communicate honestly towards the resolution of the unmet needs of yourself and your partner, you move through the wall of conflict into a deeper level of intimacy.

Consider conflict as a natural filter for your relationships. It takes courage to be honest and vulnerable with people; not every relationship makes it through the wall of conflict. Sometimes relationships may be unconsciously stuck in a loop with the parties unable to communicate their needs and the connection is destroyed. Other times, it may be the case that the parties decide the relationship is not worth the discomfort of addressing the issues.

I remember losing my temper talking with a tradesman, a friend of mine, who wasn't completing the work as he had promised. I needed him to listen to me. I let him know his work was not meeting my expectations and although he kept saying he would redo it, in the end he didn't keep his word. After weeks of pent-up disappointment and frustration, my phone conversation escalated and I was yelling so loudly that everyone in the office heard me.

As I stood there in the silent aftermath, confronted by what just happened, my chest was heaving. As I gathered my breath, I asked myself, "What the hell was that?" I had thrown away my serenity, self-respect and friendship. And for what? The paint on a door. It was ridiculous: upon reflection, it was obvious that my rage was out of proportion and had very little to do with the tradesman. I attempted to make amends with him soon after that. However, the damage had been done: he didn't trust me after the way I had treated him. I could see how the cycle of my asking over and over to be heard and never getting what I needed triggered my wound of not being heard and caused my emotional outburst. I vowed never to let that happen again.

Taking ownership of my wellbeing enables me to be conscious and clear-minded in my interactions. Gone are the days of being unconscious under the influence. Nowadays, I'm awake for my mistakes. Dealing with the tradesman, I saw the line where kindness, calm and reason ended, and I chose to jump down the rabbit hole into the "hell hath no fury" hurricane. Before that happened, a part of me had believed that I would find satisfaction in expressing myself that way. Now I know that is not true.

In my relationships today, I use anger as a spotlight to identify what I need; if the other person doesn't give me what I need, I give it to myself. When I notice I feel angry with my husband or a friend, I know it's all about me. No one else makes me angry. Rather than flip out, I take a step back to investigate and process what's going on for me. I'll contemplate, journal or do a coaching exercise to calm myself. Then I can go back to them, admit my part in the situation and do things differently. I still make mistakes in my relationships: my missteps today are what teach me about what I need and who I want to be tomorrow.

See Resources at the back of the book for Wall of Conflict Exercise.

Fun Tools

Shake It Off

Movement in the morning is magic. The morning I wrote this piece I wasn't feeling that great when I opened my eyes. I did a self check-in and noticed a lot of negative thinking contributing to my feeling crappy: I could see the writing on the wall. I remembered one of my peers reminding me that sometimes it's easier to change your physical state than your mental state, which in turn changes them both. These days my tools for doing things differently can be wacky and joyous. Emotion is energy in motion and shifting my emotions can be as simple as dancing to a song I love like Taylor Swift's "*Shake It Off.*"

Listening to Swift's lyrics makes me think of my dog Harley. I watch her shake it off a dozen times a day. She'll shake it off when she feels bad after I discipline her for trying to chase a bike. She'll even shake it off when she feels good after I give her lots of love; rubbing her belly, scratching her ears and hugging her. Whatever the emotion, Harley naturally shakes it off.

How do animals deal with the intense energy rush of life or death? Look at the behaviour of the a gazelle being chased by a lion. We know that fear triggers a fight/flight/freeze response, flooding the body with stress chemicals like cortisol and adrenaline. This temporary stress response prepares the body to address the dangerous situation. This state of high alert is meant to be temporary as increased levels of these chemicals cause damage over the long term. What does the gazelle do to alleviate this flood of fear once it escapes? It wildly shakes its body and rolls to the ground to release the energy burst. This is a natural response for animals to return to homeostasis.

Check out these websites, Total Release Experience and Pace Connections, for their perspective on using this natural response for relief in humans.

The same is true for humans. Our bodies naturally want to release the excess energy of our emotions. Think of a time when you were trying to stop yourself from crying. Maybe you hurt yourself or you were upset and you didn't want to cry in front of others. Do you recall your lip quivering before your tears rushed over you? What about feeling overly anxious and noticing your leg shaking? Perhaps you've witnessed someone vibrating after the shock of an accident. When we allow it, our bodies are set up to release the intense energy in order to protect us from what I call "frying our circuits."

What are the risks of staying stuck in the fight/flight/freeze response? The Mayo Clinic suggests that staying in the stress response state can increase your risks for the following conditions:

Anxiety
Depression
Digestive problems
Headaches
Muscle tension and pain
Heart disease, heart attack, high blood pressure and stroke
Sleep problems
Weight gain
Memory and concentration impairment

We are rarely in life or death situations; however, the stress and anxiety we feel in our body can often feel like it's life or death. We can be triggered into the fight/flight/freeze response by the fear of not paying our rent or of catching Covid. We may have angry feelings about our relationship or the war in Ukraine.

In the book *Words Can Change Your Brain*, authors Andrew Newberg and Mark Robert Waldman talk about the impact of words on your brain. Their studies show the impact of angry and fearful words. Angry words send alarm messages through the brain and partially shut down logic and reasoning centres located in the frontal lobes. Fearful words activate the amygdala fight or flight response. When we worry, if we start fantasizing about negative outcomes our brain begins working on counter-strategies and we overtax our brains by ruminating on fearful possibilities. Increase of activity in your amygdala and the release of dozens of stress-producing hormones and neurotransmitters interrupt the normal functions of your brain, especially those that are involved with logic, reason, language processing and communication.

The writers conclude that prolonged exposure to negative words and thinking can actually damage the way you regulate your memory, feelings and emotions. We've all experienced how stress, fear and anger can disrupt our sleeping and affect our appetite. Being stuck in negative words and thinking may also disrupt how your brain regulates happiness, longevity and health.

When I wrote this section, I needed to get out of a funk. I knew movement would help. Long before I read any of the research, movement made me feel better. In this instance, I did a little dance and made up a silly rap song with sounds. I acted goofy and loved it. All that jumping around with music had my brain releasing the feel-good hormones.

My husband ran screaming from the room: I didn't care. All that mattered was I felt better.

Meditation

Meditation is an essential part of self-care. When I was nineteen, there were no apps. Now we have spiritual support at our fingertips: back then you learned meditation from a teacher or a book. The first type of meditation I learned was Transcendental Meditation. We began with a sacred ceremony in which my teacher gave me a private mantra: a word that I chanted in my head. I was recommended to sit at least twenty minutes morning and night when I would chant my sacred word to calm my mind.

I have learned and practiced many types of meditation, including Zen meditation, meditations from Mother Amma, Heart Rhythm Meditation and countless guided visual meditations. A simple practice is to sit with my eyes closed and breathe into my body. I imagine opening up my crown to the cosmos with white light running down my spine and into the Earth. I put my attention on my feet and notice all the sensations in my feet on the ground. I notice my seat in the chair, my back straight against the chair with my head held high like a pharaoh, as my teacher Cheryl used to say. I raise my shoulders up to my ears, roll them back slowly and gently drop them to open my heart. I connect with the core of my self, silent with my breathing, drawing breath deep into my belly, feeling my blood pumping through my veins and energy rushing through me. Time in silence with myself and my breath is nourishing for me. I believe anything I do for myself is also nourishing for my husband, family, friends, clients and community.

Meditation is soothing for me but it took time and practice to learn. In the beginning it was difficult to sit still. My thoughts were not always pleasant or friendly. An important step to being able to sit comfortably in silence was clearing out obsessive thinking. In my coaching practice, we call it content. Think of it as little parts of you that have something to say. The more you resist their opinions, the louder they can become. For me, they were once so loud I dove into drugs and alcohol for silence. Thankfully, there is a much better way.

Clearing the negative thinking made it more comfortable to be in silence. I learned in recovery to do a Step Four to help empty years of pent-up thoughts and emotions. In my work now I use a practice called "Karma Clearing" (which I share at the end of the book). It's a practice of expressing buried thoughts and feelings around a specific subject by expressing them in a safe space or journalling about them.

In meditation, I sit in order to spend time with myself without any judgement. The fact that I've made it to the place of sitting is a celebration for me: breath is my friend and healing companion. Breathing in, I receive and breathing out, I give back to the world.

Meditation is a spiritual practice of learning to accept what is. One day of meditation, my thoughts may be all over the place; I'm constantly looking at my phone to see how much time is left. Another day, I am surprised at how smoothly it happens and how peaceful I feel. Every day, I open more and more to accepting what is, without the painful drive of perfection that once haunted me. Everyone is different, there is no right or wrong way to do it. Maybe it's counting breaths, using a mantra, using a guided meditation from your phone, walking in the forest, studying the birds outside or watching the clouds change. You find your own magic; your breath will take you there.

Breathing into this moment, I feel my nostrils inviting breath into my body. I imagine the oxygen in the air nourishing my blood and my blood nourishing all my cells. I feel my heart pumping blood all through my body, I can feel the energy passing through all my limbs and back into the earth. Focusing on my breathing in and out, I feel a part of life, a part of everything. I am grateful to be alive. My imagination takes me on a journey of gratitude for the love in my life with images of my husband, friends, family and my dog, Harley. My feelings of gratitude bring up more and more images and memories of what I am grateful for here and now.

I was inspired to host a thirty-day challenge for meditation on my group Facebook page, *Practices to Free Yourself Live Your Dreams*. There are thirty days of video called *Meditate and Feel Great Mornings* with me guiding the viewer through a simple breathing meditation. The intention was all about creating a routine. At first, we sat for five minutes and then slowly we increased our meditation time to twenty-four minutes. Everything is easier when we do it with a buddy and a video series felt like a useful virtual buddy for anyone who wanted to start meditating. Here's the link for my facebook group. You'll find the video series in the *Guides* section of the group.

See Resources at the back of the book for Karma Clearing Exercise.

Asking The Right Questions

Asking the right question is a way of taking control of your journey. "Why" questions keep you in the suffering of the problem. If you ask "Why?" you can fall down an endless cavern of painful possibilities with no answers. "Why did my father die? Why was my mother sexually assaulted? Why am I alive in recovery while my friends are dead?" There are no helpful answers.

"How" questions are about focusing on the solution, taking action and moving forward. Questions like "How can I feel better? How can I do things differently? How can this be a good thing?" shift you from "I can't do this," to "How can I do this?" and create momentum to move you forward. Thinking "I can't do this," feels like walking head first into a wall; asking yourself "How can I do this?" is like opening a door to possibility with the embedded energy of intention, "I can do it." Once I've made the decision to do it, it's already happening in my mind, and the work is uncovering the details.

When I was working as an assistant for a financial advisor, I was constantly learning new skills and programs to support our clients. The financial industry was heavily regulated with processes and paperwork continually changing. I remember being super stressed-out a lot of the time because I was new to the business and struggling with figuring things out, often feeling overwhelmed with "I can't do this."

My mentor had decades of experience that provided a history of seeing time and again that there was always a way to do whatever needed to be done. Listening to her stories, I adopted a new mantra: "There is always more than one way to do everything." After endlessly looking for the one needle in the haystack of my most recent challenge, trading in the handcuffs of a single solution for the freedom of multiple solutions relaxed my nervous system.

A critical aspect of "How can I do this?" is realizing that I don't need to know everything myself. My husband is a master of networking and he's taught me to ask myself, "Who do I know that can help?" Whenever he faces a challenge or someone approaches him for help, he consults his network for someone who has the answer or knows someone who does. Each of us has our own network that stretches far and wide like a safety net ready to catch us when we fall. Knowing that I am not alone is a tremendous relief from the old anxiety of trying to do everything on my own.

Acceptance Versus Forgiveness

I was invited to consider the concept of acceptance vs. forgiveness at a communication presentation from The Haven, a non-profit transformative learning campus in Canada. At an introductory workshop my husband and I attended, staff at The Haven talked about this in terms of communication and relationships. Let's say you have an argument with your husband because he lied to you. The old thinking was that he did something wrong and forgiveness was required to resolve the problem. The Haven offered the premise that everyone is doing the best they can and when we are doing our best, we are not doing anything wrong. Instead of forgiveness, we can use acceptance as a tool to better understand our partner and resolve the problem.

I struggled with this concept because forgiveness is a pillar in the Twelve-Step programs. Until recently, I thought it was the only way to move from resentment to serenity. I had spent years searching for ways to make forgiveness easier, contemplating ideas such as, "Forgiveness does not mean you condone what was done. It doesn't mean what happened was right or OK. Forgiveness is a gift you give yourself." What I realize now is that these concepts opened me up to acceptance and enabled forgiveness. What if acceptance was all I needed for resolution?

My experience with resentments taught me how painful they were. On the spectrum of right and wrong, I was stuck on being right. The anger and resentment I carried was a deadweight inside me that blocked the light of who I am. Once I realized the price I was paying for my indignation, I was willing to do anything to free myself, even forgive the man who hurt my mother.

Resentment is like drinking poison and hoping it will kill your enemies.

Nelson Mandela

There is so much emotion or "charge" around the idea of forgiveness. It separates people because of ingrained polarities such as these: they are right and the other is wrong, one is good and the other is bad. The emotions surrounding the polarities create a combative scenario, closing down communication and understanding.

Out beyond ideas of wrongdoing and rightdoing, there is a field. I'll meet you there.

Rumi, The Great Wagon

I see clients who are so furious about the wrong done to them they can't see straight or think clearly. They tell me that forgiveness is impossible. They are stuck because of these intense feelings with no way to get unstuck. Transforming the charge is necessary before they can accept what happened or forgive anyone.

I've noticed a significant difference between acceptance and forgiveness. Acceptance has an inherent neutrality. It's missing the intense charge forgiveness has around right and wrong. Acceptance does not require you to move through the judgement of right and wrong that forgiveness does. There seem to be fewer negative emotions to release with acceptance than forgiveness.

When clients have discharged the situation by experiencing and expressing their feelings, they see their problem in a new light. It is what it is. My Zen teacher once offered the analogy of feelings being like the weather. I am the mountain and my emotions are the weather. The mountain stays the same while the weather comes and goes. I am here while my emotions ebb and flow.

Let's go back to the example of arguing with your partner because they lied to you. When you begin communicating using the premise that they are doing the best they can and they haven't done anything wrong, it's less likely you'll be motivated by an emotional charge like anger. When you make the choice to see the situation as it is, you are focusing on the present, looking at the facts and choosing to accept what's in front of you.

Feeling calm and non-judgemental makes an open and honest dialogue more likely than an argument. While having a conversation with the intention to understand your partner rather than judging them about their wrongdoing, you may discover that they lied to you because they didn't want to disappoint you. This is a different scenario than someone lying to manipulate you or because they betrayed you. Once you've heard the backstory behind their lying, it becomes easier to understand their behaviour and move on to a mutually beneficial solution to the problem of not telling the truth. With better understanding, you can experience deeper intimacy in your ever-evolving relationship.

The Steps To Getting There

Contemplating acceptance or forgiveness of my resentments, I felt overwhelmed, having no idea where to begin. My AA sponsor told me I needed to be willing. When you are willing, you can accept anything. That's how I learned to do the Steps. In order to be free of my resentments I needed to be aware of them. In my work today, I call it "Making the unconscious conscious." It was time for Step Four from *The Big Book of AA*: "Made a searching and fearless moral inventory of ourselves."

My sponsor, Susanne, instructed me to make a list of my resentments, the person I was resentful towards, what happened, how it affected me.

This doesn't mean that you are responsible for the bad things that happened in your life or that you deserved them.

Later in the steps, I would also look at my part in the situation.

It's about being open to a different point of view. She said something like, "In every situation you have a part, even if it's only 2%." She told me I had to be willing to look for my part in every situation, and that I would probably feel pretty crappy while I was writing this list of resentments. She instructed me to do it to the best of my ability and give myself a time limit. Once my time was up, I was done.

Writing is a powerful healing tool. I had never in my life taken the time to consider all these people with such a specific formula. Putting my attention on these resentments and owning my contribution to the situation or to my suffering, I started to see patterns in my behaviour. I was astonished to see the same "defects of character" coming up time and again. The truth was as crystal clear as the blue ink on the crisp white paper in front of me.

In Step Five I told my sponsor everything I had written down. I shook as I read my list. Susanne listened to me without any judgement, holding me in an invisible hug while I poured out my heart. There were things on that paper I had never said to another living soul. It was a purging of all the poison I had held inside that had been eating away at me. I had no idea what she would say; even so, I trusted and respected her.

I told her that what happened to my mom was my fault. I felt Susanne's conviction when she locked eyes with me and told me that was bullshit; it was never my fault. That little girl never did anything wrong. I was struck with her certainty and for the first time ever, I believed that I hadn't done anything wrong.

We walked out onto her balcony and burned those pages, releasing a lifetime of pain. The cathartic ceremony filled her condo and the sky with smoke. We had been so caught up in the moment we had forgotten to close her sliding door. I cried from the relief of letting it all go, then we coughed and laughed. I felt clean from the inside out, free of all the venomous thoughts, liberated from blaming myself for something that was never my fault.

Step Six was making a list of all the character defects I uncovered with my list of resentments. Contemplating my contribution to my resentments revealed my list of defects. I used this list of behaviours for Step Seven: the exercise of asking my Higher Power to remove all my negative character traits. I needed willingness and faith to follow Step Seven's instructions: "Humbly asked Him to remove our shortcomings."

When Susanne gave me instructions for Step Eight, "Made a list of all persons we had harmed, and became willing to make amends to them all," she told me to put myself on that list and write out all the ways I had hurt myself. This was a novel idea for someone fixated on the needs of others. It would never have occurred to me to consider how I had hurt myself in my addiction.

This step teetered on unbearable for me. I had always been sensitive to the feelings of others. Pondering how my actions had hurt people tortured me. What has stuck with me all these years after creating that list are the memories of what I was thinking and feeling at the time I hurt the people on my list. Those behind-the-scenes details softened my heart towards myself and deepened my empathy for the others on my list of resentments.

Next came Step Nine: "Became willing to make amends to those we had harmed." The context for amends here is to do things differently. How could I learn from what I had done? What would I do differently? The whole exercise taught me ownership and how powerful it is to claim something. I had been powerless over other people and the things that happened to me. However, I learned that by claiming how I had contributed to the situation and making amends for my part, I could feel powerful again.

One of the names on my list came from a time when I had relations with a man who was already committed to another woman. I heard from mutual friends that his girlfriend hated me. What she didn't know was that I fell for him at a time when they had broken up. Once they were reconciled, he and I came together one last time when the two of us were drunk. It was a pathetic experience that filled me with shame. I vowed never to cheat with anyone ever again.

Amends are about taking action. I learned about making living amends the first time I did Step Nine. My first living amends were to myself and my parents, promising that I would never drink again.

When I examined my drinking behaviour, it became obvious to me how many horrible mistakes I could have avoided if I had not been drunk. Looking at the wreckage of my past was like witnessing the aftermath of a man-made disaster, like a terrorist bombing. I was overcome by the destruction caused by drinking and determined to keep it from ever happening again. This living amends is the most effective way to keep myself from repeating my past painful mistakes. If ever the thought of drinking passes through my mind, I stop myself dead in my tracks and remember the emotional demolition I caused myself and others. It keeps me from drinking every time.

> This recent in-depth article from the BBC explores new attitudes about alcohol in young people along with greater self-awareness and self-care. Reading this article I am optimistic that the next generation is learning from our mistakes.

In my coaching today, I guide clients to clear the charge around their past mistakes with an Accelerated Evolution practice called "Karma Clearing."

See Resources at the back of the book for Karma Clearing exercise.

Accepting The Devil

Contemplating making amends to everyone on my list was unnerving. Susanne, who had helped many sponsees in her then thirty-three years of sobriety, was quick to assure me with two crucial insights. The first: all I had to do was be willing to make amends. I could surrender my list to my Higher Power with the knowledge that when the time came I would know what to do and how to do it. The second: I was to separate my list into groups according to their level of difficulty.

There were two names on that list in their own category of impossible. The idea of making amends to them was beyond my comprehension at the time. Susanne reminded me that it was enough to be willing to be willing to make amends to them. I took her advice and just left them there in their special category, having faith that if and when the time came, I would know what to do.

The list of persons I had harmed included people from my list of resentments: those who had harmed me. The first name on my impossible list was that of a man whom I had begun to hate when I was a child, a man whom I haven't yet mentioned. The longer I knew that raging alcoholic, the more he hurt me and the more I saw the way he hurt others. My hatred for him grew and grew. I had no idea how to make amends for hating someone that much.

The compassion I learned to give to myself for my transgressions created insight into his behaviour. Certainly it didn't change what he had done; however, being honest about the incredible pain I had caused others with my drinking softened my heart, even for him. In the beginning, the softness for him was minimal so he stayed on the impossible list for years.

Then one day I planned a trip home to visit my family, who still lived in the city where I grew up, the same city where the man I hated lived. After the personal and spiritual development I had embraced, all the hours of prayer and meditation, I knew it was time to make amends with him. Still, it was like watching the movie of my life; I was on the edge of my seat wondering how this would unfold. As the trip drew nearer, I slowly surrendered to the idea of making amends.

Even when I made the decision to go to his house, I still wasn't clear on exactly what would happen. All I had was my willingness and my faith that it would work out and that I would be guided to do the right thing.

I had always thought of him with disgust. When I was young and forced to be around him, my actions, tone of voice and comments were all dripping with disdain. Once I was old enough to control how and where I spent my time, I did everything possible not to be around him. When it was time to make amends, I had been alcohol-free for a number of years and had completed Steps Four, Eight and Nine enough times to feel capable of making amends to him. I understood myself and the world in a completely different way than was possible when I first decided he was someone I owed amends.

When my husband and I went to visit him, he was dying of cancer. We sat at the kitchen table and still I had no idea what the amends would be. I don't remember the conversation; I remember sitting with him practicing love and acceptance. I noticed his frailty. It wasn't just his pale complexion or the way his clothes hung loosely on him. It was his spirit. It felt like he was disappearing. The powerful, roaring bully whose energy used to jolt me as a child, whom I constantly belittled as an adult, was gone.

For the first time in a long time, I didn't struggle to be kind to him. I sat with him, wishing him well, free of all the hatred and judgement that had once weighed me down. I had been fierce in my determination that he was bad and wrong. As I sat there after my own struggles with addiction, it was clear that he was only human. I chose to accept him as he was. My amends to him was to be kind. It sounds simple, yet I can tell you that the feeling of hatred that used to be a black hole sucking my life energy had been replaced. At last I felt peace. Peace born from the deep understanding of the truth that he was doing the best he could.

The revelation had only become possible after examining my own wrongdoings. Once I had the courage to feel the pain, shame and guilt for the ways I had hurt myself and others, I had the unique perspective of the perpetrator. Being willing to explore what I had done, along with what I was feeling inside as I hurt others, opened my heart with a new level of compassion. I was able to accept myself as doing the best I could. That was the foundation for nurturing a capacity to accept the same, even in the most horrendous individual.

We will not regret the past nor wish to shut the door on it.

Alcoholics Anonymous

In the 1930s, when *The Big Book of AA* was written, the meaning of regret was different than it is today. The meaning then: not repeating our mistakes. We will not repeat the past. That definition made far more sense to me than today's common meaning for regret: to be very sorry for mistakes.

My practice today is about remembering the mistakes I made as learning tools rather than ways to punish myself. Being willing to look at how I contributed to my resentments and admitting my mistakes gave me the ability to separate the actions from the person. We do this with children all the time; they are not bad kids, they just did a bad thing. I learned how to have compassion for all the things I did. My self-compassion taught me to love and accept the person I was. Doing that for myself has opened my heart for even more love and acceptance of others.

I never saw that man again. The next time I went home to visit my family was for his funeral. It was a lovely day in October, warm enough to be outside with no coat. I stood on the grass listening to all these strangers share passionately about the kindness and generosity of the man. There was story after story full of love and admiration for him and how his help had changed their lives.

It was bizarre to witness how one man could be so many different things to so many people. I struggled with the thought, "Are they talking about the same person?" until I settled into the authenticity of their gratitude for him. At the time, it felt like I was in an episode of *The Twilight Zone*. Was he a devil, an angel or just human? The choice was up to me.

It makes me smile when I think about what I learned. Looking back now, I see it was one of those moments that proved I didn't know everything. As a child I had been convinced he was the devil. Turns out even the devil does good deeds. As an adult I've experienced enough to see life through shades of grey instead of the black and white windows of my childhood.

The Face Of Your Enemy

Cybil was on my amends list after the breakup of our friendship. One of my closest friends, she suddenly began distancing herself from me. I approached her many times to discuss what was bothering her and her reply was always, "Nothing." I loved her so much and I was willing to do whatever needed to be done to repair our friendship; however, she didn't seem to feel the same.

While I was still drinking, our group of friends went on a big trip to New York. Cybil and I were roommates for all our trips, and I was looking forward to days full of adventure and nights full of deep conversation and laughter. This trip was nothing like the others. She was distant and cold, treating me like the enemy. Soon I noticed that everyone in our group was angry with me and I had no idea what I had done. Needless to say, the trip was terribly uncomfortable. When I returned home, Chris, another member of the group, called me to clear the air. I found out that they were angry because Cybil had been talking about me behind my back. She had bombarded them with stories of my erratic behaviour and cruelty to her. As Chris provided examples of her stories, I discredited each one until he appreciated they were all a lie. The two of us were shocked by Cybil's manipulation. I hung up the phone confused, betrayed and furious.

Around that time I had the good fortune to meet a Zen Master who agreed to take me on as a student and help me with my struggles. I have always been curious about different spiritual practices and was excited to explore new tools and perspectives. Meanwhile, I continued to obsess about this betrayal. I was so angry, I couldn't sleep. Our group used to be like family, spending holidays together, going on trips, supporting each other through any hardship. I kept playing our conversations over and over in my head, remembering all I had done for her during our friendship. How dare she cast me out!

My Zen teacher shared an ancient practice of using the face of my enemy. She instructed me to imagine putting Cybil's face on my face and seeing this experience through her eyes.

Walk a mile in my shoes...
See what I see
Hear what I hear
Feel what I feel
Then maybe you'll understand
Why I do what I do
Until then don't judge me

Unknown
Inspired by Mary T. Lathrap's poem "Judge Softly," 1895

Looking through the eyes of my enemy to experience her point of view was a profound experience. I had been so fixated on my own righteous anger it hadn't occurred to me to consider her side. I was too busy running around telling anyone who would listen about this terrible woman and her painful betrayal. With my Zen Master's guidance, it was time for me to be honest with myself about how I had contributed to the destruction of our friendship. When I pondered where the separation began, I remembered that she had started treating me differently after a party where I got blackout drunk.

There was a man in our group she was interested in so we had decided to throw a party as a way for her to get to know him. Everyone was drinking profusely and we all became inebriated quickly. He had come to the party with no idea that she liked him. He began flirting with me. Being drunk, I had forgotten our plan so I enjoyed his attention, which upset my friend a great deal. Once I realized this, I did my best to convince him that my friend was a much better match for him and apologized to Cybil for my inappropriate behaviour.

However, the damage had been done. She never trusted me again.

The practice of embodying Cybil's point of view by putting her face on my face had a visceral effect on me. There had been a lot of prayers asking to be relieved of my anger and to accept what she had done. Being willing to consider her feelings and motivations took me behind her actions and into her heart. It was an exercise that revealed her pain and suffering in a way that enabled deeper comprehension of her actions. At last I could accept what she had done and was relieved of my fury and feelings of betrayal.

With the help of my Zen Master, I chose to learn from the incident. The amends I made to Cybil: never to act that way with any other friend. We met again years later, an encounter Chris set up. I remember being nervous before I got there, worried about what to say and concerned about what she might say or do. Once we were in each other's presence, we quickly grasped that each of us had made peace with what happened. We exchanged our different life stories, then moved from nervousness to comfort and even laughter. I was grateful to notice I was happy to hear all her news and wish her well. I believed she felt the same for me.

Learning this practice of putting the face of another on my face was also valuable at my job. I often used it when I was on the phone, listening to customer questions and complaints. I have always been a great listener and knew it was necessary to hear them out before we could work on a solution. However, I was stressed by my internal tension between them wanting to talk and my fixation on getting a resolution so I could return to the mountain of work on my desk.

Practicing this empathetic action moved me from the internal stress of "wishing they would just hurry up" to a calm desire to understand what they were going through. Having their face on my face allowed me to relax and let go of my agenda. My clients felt heard and we found solutions more quickly than before. As a coach, I often take my clients through a similar practice, and they are amazed by the insights and peace that arise from opening their heart to feel the issue from another's point of view.

Inner Voice: Friend Or Foe?

We all have our own inner wisdom to carry us through challenges. This is the voice that will encourage you to try new things, the voice that soothes you when you're scared or worried. It's the voice that leads you to a book or a person when you need help: your intuition, soul voice or guidance. The critic, on the other hand, is the one that is always questioning in a negative way, criticizing, belittling, berating, judging, anything that makes you feel worse about yourself.

While I was writing this, I recognized that my perspective on the critic has changed. In the past, that inner critic was the master of my torture, dolling out emotional, spiritual and physical pain. Now that I accept my emotions as messengers rather than persecutors, I can see the critic in a new light as well. It occurred to me that in the past I didn't always listen to soft, kind words. What if I needed to have brutal, angry, painful words to get my attention?

We've all had that teacher who was a severe disciplinarian. I remember my elementary school principal, a former army officer who often shocked me into paying attention by slamming his pointer on my desk or the junior high Math teacher who scared the crap out of me with a piercing glare and demoralizing comments. I didn't enjoy their teaching style and I wouldn't recommend it. Still, the fact remains that their attention motivated my accomplishment. I was the most outstanding student in my elementary school and the second runner-up for most outstanding student in my junior high school.

My parents were also strong disciplinarians whom I constantly rebelled against. As a child, I couldn't reconcile their rigidity. As an adult, I know through my experience, exploration, and enlightening conversations with my dad that behind every single action that seemed harsh to me was deep love. What if our inner critic has exactly the same intention?

A Course in Miracles says, "Everything is love or a call for love." What if your inner critic is simply trying a different angle to reach you? If the job of the critic is to motivate change for your awakening and you are motivated by pain, then it is simply doing its job. I've spent years motivated by pain. That lesson is complete. I have graduated from the school of "That which doesn't kill you makes you stronger," and I see now that my inner critic was a key player in my transformation. Hero or villain is all a matter of perception. Today I choose the mantra, "Everything is happening for my awakening."

A New Way Of Living

On the lower levels of awareness there are no solutions, on the higher levels of awareness, no problems.

Roberto Assagiolli, Italian Psychologist

Accelerated Evolution has facilitated the most significant change in me since I quit drinking. I comprehend myself as an energetic being and navigate the energy in myself and others for our awakening. The emotions that once terrified me have become the harbingers of power and wisdom. This work has connected me with the profound peace and joy of who I am. I am light, and my intention is to share my gifts in service.

You Run The Narrative

In *Scandal*, a recent TV show, Kerry Washington played a political spin doctor or fixer named Olivia Pope. Clients came to her with scandals; she would create their public relations strategy. Her focus was to "Run the narrative." She and her clients wanted to be the first in the press with their point of view in order to influence public opinion.

Like this public relations expert, you run the narrative in your life. How you choose to perceive the events of your life determines how you feel and therefore how you behave. The stories you tell yourself create your reality. Think about it. What's a story you tell yourself over and over?

A story I consciously choose everyday is "I am taken care of." This is my antidote for years of feeling unsafe. This belief was part of my thinking long before I became a coach. It's a statement of faith that I hold onto when life gets shaky, and a confirmation of fact when something happens to look after me in a way I could not have imagined on my own.

For example, I was twenty-something and flat broke. I grabbed a jacket I hadn't worn in a while and put my hand in my pocket. There I found an uncashed pay cheque. That cheque was a godsend back then. For me to go from $0 to $175 was a miracle.

Another time that demonstrated the Universe was taking care of me came after a big fight with my common-law boyfriend. He had stayed out all night doing who-knows-what when I thought he was working. I was furious after spending my evening tossing and turning, worried sick about him, instead of sleeping. We were on opposite schedules, me working days and him working nights so it took two or three days to find a time for us to have a conversation. Once that happened, I exploded all over him because he was lying and I knew it. It was a brutal exchange. There was no consideration on my part, no calm, no kindness, only me screaming, judging and accusing all at once. The poor guy didn't stand a chance. After three days of seething, I was furious and he ended up wearing all the anger and resentment, as well as a plate I flung in his direction. Well, he dodged the plate. I wouldn't say he was totally innocent; however, there was no room for any kind of adult exchange when I was yelling and throwing things at him. Needless to say, he didn't stick around for much longer. As soon as he saw his exit, he slipped out quietly behind my back.

Once I calmed myself down with a drink, gathered my thoughts and was ready for a reasonable conversation, I went into the bedroom to discover he had packed a bag and left. I was screwed since he was the majority breadwinner in our household. I sat there ruminating in my living room with my Crown Royal on ice, in shock, when the phone rang.

"Hello?"

"This is so and so from TD Canada Trust. I'm calling to let you know that your Gold Mastercard is ready." Just like that, my expenses were covered by an unrequested credit card.

Running the narrative is a crucial part of sustainable change. When we transform our thinking, which transforms our experience, we need to ground the new information, the new learning, as our new thinking. The way to do this is to make it part of our current story. When we think about the negative emotion (charge) or experiences and talk about them, it's important that we tell the story of the old feeling or behaviour in the past tense and name it as old behaviour: What happened to me... I used to think or feel... In the past I would react this way...I remember when I used to...What I used to tell myself was...

Looking at it this way, we claim the transformation and new behaviour by telling the new story in the present tense. "Today, I do this... Now I behave this way... I AM..." The way we think and speak about our experiences informs our beliefs, behaviour and our lives. What we focus on expands. When we think and talk about our negative past experiences in the present tense, they continue to impact our lives negatively. On the other hand, when we think and talk about negative past experiences in the past tense and choose thoughts and words to reframe the experience in a positive light, we change our lives for the better. We claim a contemporary perspective and our new narrative empowers us to create a new reality.

The words I AM are powerful tools of manifestation. I coach my clients to use these words to claim their new reality. They create lasting transformations with statements like these:

I am confident.
I am loveable.
I am honouring my body and spirit.
I am powerful.
I am enough.

I recently created the powerful claim statement: "I am a skier." I love skiing; it is one of the few sports I did well with and enjoyed as a kid. When I was looking for something fun to do with my husband, I thought of skiing. The first time we went skiing this year I was primed to do well. My husband and I had a bet on how many times I would fall. If I fell more than four times he won. Four times or less, I won.

It was a beautiful day with incredible powder. The problem was I had no idea how to ski well in powder. When I fell at the beginning of the first run, I could see the writing on the wall. To my utter dismay, I fell nine times that day. The only good thing about it was that my husband made some money. I was determined to do better on our next trip, asking myself, "How can I do this differently? What's the experience I want to have?" My backside was killing me from a spectacular wipe-out on our last run the Eagle chair that day and I most certainly didn't want a repeat of that beauty of a bruise on my butt. I know better than to try and solve the problem with the mind that created the problem so I went out and talked with my friends to find the solution.

My friend shared that the majority of ski injuries happen in the afternoon on the last run of the day. That was my experience. My plan for the next trip was to try the more difficult runs early in the day. After the pain of the fall, part of me was scared to ski again, scared of falling. I knew I had to shift my mindset around falling to prevent history repeating itself.

Accelerated Evolution to the rescue. I processed the fear around falling and after getting to a higher state of consciousness, I had beneficial visions explaining the importance of falling for me. Falling is necessary to being a good skier. What I learn from my falls informs all the times I stand up on my skis. There will always be times when falling is the best option for me. If I was flying in the direction of a tree, falling would be the only way to save myself from harm. Life is full of polarities like up and down, and they need each other to exist. How would you understand *fall* without *stand*?

At the end of a session, I ask myself and my clients, "What's your new narrative?" We want to embody the insights from their session with a concise sentence expressing their new way of thinking. In this case, I was looking for my claim statement and came up with something like, "I am open to skiing." At the time, that seemed to encompass my learning around the harmony between falling and standing up. However, once I was on the ski hill, feeling relaxed without any fear in my body, the lights went on and I heard my true claim statement: "I am a skier!" What that means to me is that whatever the details, the fact is that I am a skier. I do what a skier does. At times I am confident, fearless, and when needed, I am observant and cautious. Can you feel the power? That's my new narrative. I am a skier.

I used my claim statement to focus on my goal rather than on any negative outcome. When I went down an advanced run by mistake and I was in over my head, I reminded myself, "I am a skier. I do what a skier does. My body knows what to do." I gave myself permission to fall when it was in my best interest, like when two people cut in front of me and I lost my balance while slowing down to avoid a collision. Being relaxed on the hill, taking my time and enjoying the scenery rather than fixating on the fear of losing control resulted in a lot more fun than I had on my previous trips. We did nine runs that day and I had one and a half falls. That's one and a half, not two.

Wonder

Wonder: all it takes is a smile, more like a grin with the intention to be playful and the desire for fun. I consciously make space for more time to play in my life. I admire a particular belly dancer who is a creative force: gorgeous, flirtatious and totally playful. Her movement is joyful and flowing, reminding me of Peter Pan's Tinkerbell, a muse awakening a different side of the brain to unleash joy, curiosity, creativity, pleasure and wonder.

Wonder – a feeling of surprise mingled with admiration, caused by something beautiful, unexpected, unfamiliar, or inexplicable

Google

Wonder takes the whole body to the moment of awe when you're looking up with big eyes, breathing slowly, completely relaxed. Thinking of wonder, I see a picture of Disney's Alice in Wonderland in her baby-blue and white dress. She is innocent and open, free of agenda, available for whatever happens because she is totally in the present, without expectation. All is surrendered to what is and there is no contemplation, analyzing or planning, only a complete expansion into what's happening now.

Your New Narrative

The way we talk to ourselves and others creates our story and shapes our reality. When you have the courage to feel through your painful past to a new perception, the sustainability of your transformation depends on you holding onto your new story with every fibre of your being. You have the power to maintain your massive shift by focusing on your new thinking and using your language to create your new narrative. In *Words Can Change Your Brain*, the authors propose that over time, it's possible to change how your disturbing memories are stored. By speaking about negative memories in a relaxed and positive way over and over, the positive words become encoded with the memory, which affects how the brain recalls them.

I put my tragedy and its power into the past by creating a new story. I'm telling you here about my experience and its impact in the past tense. It is the old story, my old way of thinking. The words make a difference. Saying that I used to feel trapped or that it used to have power over me reinforces that is no longer the case.

Using your thoughts and imagination, you are writing the script of a movie called life. Imagine you are the master of your own destiny with the ability to create the story for what happens and reshape the story of your past. Satyen's teacher, Zivorad Slavinski, called the mind a "meaning-making machine." You have the power to decide what things mean in your life.

Today, I feel different in my body when I think about witnessing my mother's assault. I know what happened but all the pain around it is gone. Today, the story I choose to focus on is what I learned from what happened.

I am a powerful being today because of my past. That's it. I decide how I use that experience to shape who I am today. I choose to see what happened as the building blocks for the extraordinary person I am.

I cannot change the past. I absolutely, 100%, have the power to choose the way I think about the past. In recovery, I often hear people say they are a grateful alcoholic. I didn't understand that for a long time. Then one day I was contemplating my life and how happy I was living alcohol-free. I was amazed at the spiritual growth in myself. I recognized that I was a stronger, smarter, kinder person because of the things I learned and practiced in recovery. That's when it hit me. I too am grateful for the experiences I had as an alcoholic and drug addict. I would not be who I am today without the misery I suffered as an addict. Only when I bottomed out and became desperate enough to do things differently did I transform my life.

When I was drinking, I hated myself and often pushed away anyone who cared about me. I was on my own and doomed to destroy myself. Listening to my coach, Thelma, and going to AA, I learned the tools I needed to turn my life around. I changed my job, my friends, my focus, and I got healthy physically, emotionally and spiritually. This is my practice now. This is what made me strong enough to look at the intense experience from my childhood once I found the right teachers. Now I see the tragedy itself as a powerful teacher.

When I quit drinking, it became possible to change my thinking because I stopped poisoning myself. Without drugs and alcohol in my body, I could at last think with a clear head. Recovery demanded that I take an honest look at myself and my behaviour. Once I took ownership of my thinking and behaviour, I was able to take charge of my life. I can only change one person in this life and that is me. What an empowering place to be! At last, I was awake and ready to let go of the victim mindset. Today, I embrace my power of choice, and practice living my life conscious that whatever happens in this moment is for my highest good.

All of my transformations have unfolded because of the generous support in my life. It took me many years to understand that it is OK to ask for help. I didn't fully embody the concept that asking for help was healthy until I went to AA. Once I believed it was true, I began asking for help more regularly. In recovery, Twelve-Step programs gave me permission to choose a God of my understanding and I gave myself permission to create new spiritual beliefs that supported my empowerment. Today I have the support of an amazing husband, incredible friends and colleagues, my wonderful family, along with my masters, guides, angels, God, Goddess, Universe... I believe there is limitless, loving support for myself and all of us.

When my mother was sexually assaulted, there was no way I could have imagined that being there when it happened was for my highest good. That event sent me on a lifelong journey, searching for ways to feel better. That included everything from writing, meditation, yoga, and recovery, to Accelerated Evolution. Today I see a crystal-clear path from what happened to my mom to hating men and distrusting life to growing strength and empathy, hearing stories of other survivors, from being addicted to drugs and alcohol to finding recovery, and, at last, to accepting my emotions as messengers with my highest good at heart.

I see it all as one thread: practicing living an alcohol-free life, cultivating a spiritual path, prayer and meditation, supporting my mom and family through her cancer and death, a trip to Italy and meeting Aurora, moving from experiencing tragedy as a block to choosing to see the tragedy as a gift, releasing the intense experience with Accelerated Evolution, embracing my mission to use what happened to me to help others. (take a breath) I cannot choose what happened to me in the past. I absolutely can choose how I think about it. My life up to this moment is a series of choices that has led me to a joyous and peaceful place.

My new narrative is that I am proud to be me. I am an empath with exceptional communication skills, a born cheerleader with x-ray vision into people's greatest strengths, guiding them out of the bondage of their past toward an extraordinary life. We are all diamonds who exist because of the intense transforming pressures of what we've experienced. We can choose to let the experiences define us or choose to define the experiences for ourselves. Every breath is a new opportunity for a fresh perspective.

I had no idea I would be making friends with the Boogeyman when I set out on my journey inward. I am grateful for all the souls who held my hand along the way, giving me the strength, courage and guidance to accept the most terrifying parts of myself. Learning to love all these parts of me, I watched my construct of a terrifying monster created to destroy me dissolve into a loving part of me. Ultimately, everything I've experienced in my life has been for my awakening.

I am the storyteller of my life and my story today is:

Transformation is beautiful.

You are a brilliant soul more powerful than any events from your past. Your choice to be the victim or the hero shapes the story of your life.

What's your new story?

Heidi Smith - Transformation Guide

*If you change the way you look at things,
the things you look at change.*

Wayne Dyer

Whatever has happened in the past, you can free yourself and live your dreams.

Work with me to move through the emotions blocking your desires to feel new clarity, peace and joy. Change your thinking and learn to channel your true power into accepting and enjoying all you have and all you are. Imagine the serenity of relaxing in your body and feeling safe in the world. It is absolutely possible and I can show you how. You need three things for a successful transformation:

*The willingness to explore your feelings and try something new.
The commitment to take action now.
The belief that better is possible.*

You are not alone. I am here for you. Read success stories from my clients at www.heidicoach.com

 Schedule your complimentary call with me and begin your transformation today.

Discussion & Journalling Questions

1. The author discusses emotions as "Energy in Motion." What does this concept mean to you?

2. Remember a time when you held onto a resentment about someone or something. Now remember a time when you were able to accept the wrongdoing and let it go easily. Describe how you felt in each situation. What did you do differently in the two scenarios?

3. How has reading this book changed your perspective on your emotions? What's good about that for you? What's good about this for others?

4. The author shares about how learning to ask for and accept help from others changed her life. What is your experience with requesting assistance? Describe your current support systems. Is there anything you would change?

5. The author describes the impact of different words on our thoughts and feelings along with how they contribute to our perception of our reality. Do you agree or disagree with her position? Describe your experience when using angry or fearful words. What's your experience when using loving and peaceful words? Describe how the different scenarios feel in your body. What differences do you notice in your perception?

6. Your attention is a powerful force for creating the experience you desire: "What you focus on expands." What are some of the ways you shift your focus when you notice yourself fixated on the negative? Did you learn any new tools for shifting your attention in this book? What are they?

7. Name three undesirable aspects in your life that occupy your attention.

8. Describe three desirable aspects you would rather focus on today.
9. How can you shift your attention to what you want?
10. The author stresses the importance of your "New Narrative" and how our experience is shaped by the stories we tell ourselves. An important part of transformation is claiming a new story to sustain your current thinking and solidify your evolution. After reading this book, have you noticed any stories you feel are negatively impacting you? How would you rather feel? Beliefs are thoughts we tell ourselves over and over. What's a new story you could tell yourself to cultivate how you want to feel?
11. Did reading certain parts of this book make you feel uncomfortable? If yes, what were the parts and how did you feel about them? If your feelings are messengers, what is their message for you?
12. Did reading this book lead to a new understanding or awareness of some aspect of your life? What is it?
13. What do you see as the primary message of this book?
14. How did you feel after reading this book?
15. The author shares about how doing things differently grounds our epiphanies. Share three actions you will take to demonstrate your insights from this book.

Resources

Coming into the present moment

When I had struggled with anxiety that could escalate into panic, a simple tool I learned was to put my attention on my breath and use my senses to bring me into the present moment. Looking at my hands and clenching and unclenching my fists, feeling my feet on the ground, moving them, squeezing my arms. Paying attention to my breathing and noticing these sensations, along with telling myself over and over I'm ok, in this moment I'm ok, calmed me down. Below are more exercises to bring you into the present moment which will calm you and reduce stress.

Relax The Panic

If you find yourself in panic, or freezing up, you can use this simple technique I learned from Artie Vipperla to quickly relax again.

In a seated position with a straight spine and your feet on the ground, pay attention to your breath. While breathing at a normal pace:

Turn your hips to the right, keeping your feet pointed forward.
Leaving your hips to the right, turn your ribs to the left.
Leaving your ribs to the left, turn your shoulders to the right
Leaving your shoulders to the right, turn your head to the left
Leaving your head to the left, turn your eyes to the right.
Relax your body coming back to centre.
Repeat the other way. You need only do this a few times.

Boxed Breathing

This is a simple practice of using mindful breathing to calm your body and relax your mind.

1. Exhale to a count of four.
2. Hold your lungs empty for a four-count.
3. Inhale to a count of four.
4. Hold the air in your lungs for a count of four.
5. Exhale and repeat until you feel calm.

5-4-3-2-1 Coping Technique

This technique uses all 5 senses to bring your back to the present moment if you are feeling stressed. Begin by noticing your breath.

5: Acknowledge FIVE things you see around you. It could be your phone, a cup, your computer, anything in your surroundings.

4: Acknowledge FOUR things you can touch around you. It could be your leg, your chair, or the floor under your feet.

3: Acknowledge THREE things you hear. Maybe it's the garbage truck, the fridge, your dog snoring. Focus on things you can hear outside of your body.

2: Acknowledge TWO things you can smell. Maybe you are in your office and you smell coffee, if you use scented lotion or perfume, smell your skin. Maybe you have fresh flowers at home or maybe you step outside to smell something in nature.

1: Acknowledge ONE thing you can taste. What does the inside of your mouth taste like—toothpaste or tea, maybe onion from lunch?

Six Bullet Points (changing your point of view)

THANK YOU, AURORA WINTER, FOR THIS PRACTICE

Write out six turning points in your life as bullet points. Go with the first things that come up. Don't censor or judge what arises, go with your first instinct. Just the facts, no detail or embellishment. For example: Moved to LA, First job as an architect, My daughter was born, Car accident, Mother died...

Now, tell the story of your six bullet points from the point of view of a victim. A kind of "Woe is me, I had it so hard" story, depicting the "facts" of your bullet points from a victim's outlook. Give yourself a time limit of no more than twenty minutes.

Next, give your story a catchy title that summarizes it. For example, "Burnt Out at 40, Angry and Addicted, Scared and Overweight in Vancouver..."

Now tell your six bullet points as a Hero's story. What was good about what happened? What did you learn? How are you a better person because of what you went through? Give yourself a time limit of no more than twenty minutes.

Give your Hero's story a catchy title that summarizes it. For example "Finding Passion & Purpose at 41, Empathy is my Superpower, Happy & Healthy in Vancouver..."

What are you more aware of after this practice?

What did you learn doing this exercise?

What is something good that happened to/for you as a result of doing this practice?

How will the things you've learned in this practice help others?

How do you think differently after this practice? What's your new story?

How will you apply this new awareness in your life? List 3 action steps.

Applying PHALT

1. Consider a time when you have been in pain and it was adversely affecting your day. Name three ways you can care for yourself when you're in pain.
   a.
   b.
   c.
2. Consider a time when you have been hungry and it was adversely affecting your day. Name three ways you can care for yourself when you are hungry or ways to prepare and avoid hunger and low blood sugar.
   a.
   b.
   c.
3. Consider a time when you have been angry and it was adversely affecting your day. Name three ways you can address feelings of anger.
   a.
   b.
   c.
4. Consider a time when you have been lonely and it was adversely affecting your day. Name three ways you can care for yourself when you're feeling lonely.
   a.
   b.
   c.

5. Consider a time when you have been tired and it was adversely affecting your day. Name three ways you can care for yourself when you're feeling tired.
   a.
   b.
   c.

Using The Wall of Conflict

1. The author discusses using anger as an alert to check in with yourself. Consider a recent disagreement with a friend or loved one:
   a. What was your unmet need?
   b. What was the unmet need of the other?
   c. Was there a resolution? If so, what was it?
   d. What is your new understanding of the situation when you consider the disagreement through the lens of the wall of conflict?

Karma Clearing Exercise

THANK YOU, SATYEN RAJA, FOR THIS PRACTICE

Integrity Dyads

This is a powerful exercise I learned in Accelerated Evolution that I do in workshops to uncover feelings and limiting beliefs around subjects like money, power or relationship. This is a clearing exercise to show you where you are, what's not working for you and what you want to do differently. In my workshops, participants do this in groups of two. You can also do this as a journalling exercise.

When you do this with a partner, it is called a Dyad. A Dyad is a formal communication for the purpose of understanding. It is not a conversation. You do not need to agree with the other person. Your focus is to listen with the intention to understand. There is a listening partner and a speaking partner. The listening partner will give the instructions below and listen to the speaking partner without interrupting them. As the listening partner, you put your attention on the speaking partner and listen to them without judgement. When they have finished speaking and you understand them, you reply, "Thank you," and nothing else.

If you do not understand what your partner has said, there are three communication aids you may use as the listening partner. Since this is a formal communication exercise rather than a conversation, we use formal terms that feel neutral and minimally interrupt the flow of the speaker:

"Say Again" - if you didn't hear the speaking partner.

"Clarify That" - if you didn't understand the speaking partner.

"Summarize That" - if the speaking partner has given you a lot of information and you're not sure you understand. This invites the speaking partner to consider what they've said and provide a concise statement. It's an opportunity for both of you to better understand what's been said.

The listening partner will give the instructions for both Dyads below to the speaking partner. Then you will switch roles.

It is most beneficial to spend at least twenty minutes but not more than forty-five minutes at a time with these exercises. People tend to get fatigued if they do this longer than forty-five minutes.

I recommend making a note of what you would do differently to capture what you've learned.

See next page for instructions.

Instructions

You can run these three-part Dyads on subjects like relationships, money, love, sex, drinking, addiction etc. Fill in the blank below with your subject.

Dyad One
‣ Regarding _____, **tell me something you've done** that you think you should not have done.
‣ Tell me how that affected yourself and others.
‣ Tell me what you would do differently now.

Dyad Two
‣ Regarding _____, **tell me something you failed to do** that you think you should have done.
‣ Tell me how that affected yourself and others.
‣ Tell me what you would do differently now.

Accelerated Evolution

 Learn about the methods of Accelerated Evolution 360 (AE360): The Breakthrough Experience and 8 Week Training Course + The 5 Day Live Hands-on Training + Lifetime Access to Ongoing Mastery and Training.

Websites

Alcoholics Anonymous
www.aa.org

Aurora Winter
www.aurorawinter.com

Angela Thurston
www.angelathurston.com

Cheryl Stelte
Star of Divine Light Institute: Healing & Empowerment Training
www.starofdivinelight.com

Diane Burton
https://www.themastersmasterpiece.com

Junie Swadron
https://junieswadron.com

Myo Clinic Victoria
www.myoclinic.ca

About The Illustrator

Emily Rain Verscheure is a Vancouver Island entrepreneur specializing in digital art. Alongside her trusty digital pencil, she aspires to become one of the most visionary, impactful and celebrated digital artists on the planet. She can be found at www.emilyrain.com

About The Author

Heidi Smith is a Transformation Guide. Her mission is to help others expand abundance, peace, joy and love beyond their expectations. She is an Accredited Accelerated Evolution Coach who studied under founder Satyen Raja, trainer for globally-renowned thinkers including T. Harv Eker, Colin Sprake and Gabor Mate. Heidi is a dedicated member of the training team at the Accelerated Evolution Academy. She is passionate about coaching one-on-one and in workshops where she shares practical tools and experiential techniques, empowering others to awaken their leader within to share their gifts with the world. She inspires others to live an extraordinary life, using personal and candid stories of integrating intense childhood experiences, anxiety and addiction in order to reclaim her power. She lives on Vancouver Island with husband Rob and their happy Havanese, Harley. Heidi delights in being by the ocean, sharing a delicious meal, hiking with friends and trying new things.

Find out more about Heidi at www.heidicoach.com

Lightning Source UK Ltd.
Milton Keynes UK
UKHW020953050123
414865UK00011B/1431